WHERE DO
WE
GO
FROM HERE?

ROSIE RUSHTON

Hyperion Paperbacks for Children
New York

CONTENTS

1
Party Lines

"I am not all sure," said Chelsea Gee, piling her chestnut curls into a knot on the top of her head, "that this is such a good idea."

"The hair?" queried Laura, peering over her shoulder into the mirror of the ladies' room of Gee Whiz, the restaurant owned by Chelsea's dad, and applying her third layer of Pink Persuasion lip gloss. "I think it looks cool."

"Not the hair," corrected Chelsea, spritzing it with spray gel. "Tonight. Here. With them." She jerked her head towards the restaurant door, from behind which came a peal of high-pitched laughter, followed by the chink of glasses.

Chelsea winced. "I should have known it would be a disaster," she said. "We should have gone straight to the disco—it's all your fault."

"Mine?" expostulated Laura. "How do you make that out?"

"It was you who went all gushy when my mum suggested that we all had supper here before going to The Stomping Ground," complained Chelsea. "What was it?—'Oh brilliant, Mrs. Gee, that would be so cool.' "

Another burst of laughter resonated from the restaurant.

"Cool indeed," muttered Chelsea. "Anything that involves my mother, a gang of her friends, and several bottles of red wine has the potential to be a disaster."

"I didn't know it was going to be a parents-come-too thing, did I?" reasoned Laura. "And anyway, we're escaping to The Stomping Ground in a couple of hours. It won't be so bad."

"Not for you, maybe—at least your mother is normal, and not likely to make a total idiot of herself."

"Normal? My mother?" spluttered Laura, blotting her lips with a tissue. "Would you mind telling me what is normal about a woman who appears to have lost the power of rational speech and spends all day saying things like, 'Who's a lubberly wickle chubbychops boy, den?' and pretending to be a Teletubby. Honestly, they tell you that there are risks in having a baby when you are over the hill, but they don't say that going ga-ga is one of them."

Chelsea grinned. "Mine managed the ga-ga bit without giving birth," she said. "At least you got a cute brother out of it. He is so wicked."

"Don't you start!" admonished Laura. "What with Mum fussing over him and Melvyn preparing him for university by reading the *Times* to him every night, I've had my fill of baby adoration."

"The *Times*?" queried Chelsea.

"According to Melvyn, it will broaden his vocabulary. Mind you, with a mother like mine, he needs all the linguistic help he can get. Maybe I should write some kids' stories for him when I've finished the novel."

"If you wait that long, Charlie will be at uni," laughed Chelsea.

Laura had been writing a novel since primary school. It featured a hero and heroine, prevented from consummating their passion because of dark and terrible secrets in their past. Laura was at pains to explain to anyone who asked that she couldn't write about things she hadn't done, and that the book would be finished as soon as she had first-hand experience of giving herself over to Romantic Love.

"Yes, well unfortunately, Romantic Love," she said ruefully, layering mascara on to her eyelashes, "is something that is sadly lacking in my life right now."

"What about Jon?" Chelsea asked in surprise, perching on a stool while she waited for Laura to finish her make-up. "You two haven't split, have you?"

"No," shrugged Laura. "He's really sweet and all that, and I like him a lot—but nothing happens anymore."

Chelsea nearly fell off the stool. "*Anymore?*" she gasped. "You mean—you can't mean you did—well, did *it?*"

Laura sighed in exasperation and rammed her mascara wand back in her make-up bag. "No, silly, of course we didn't!" she snapped. "It's just that when he kisses me or holds my hand, I don't go all weak at the knees and tingly anymore. And he's not very romantic—do you know what he gave me for Christmas?"

"Perfume? Chocolates?"

"If only—no, a book of cartoons, and half of them weren't even funny." She sighed. "I want the sort of guy who likes to lie in the long grass and read John Donne."

"John who?"

"The poet, stupid," said Laura. "Honestly, I am surrounded by total ignoramuses. Is it any wonder my muse is stifled? I need someone who understands my creative urges."

Chelsea burst out laughing. "You need someone who idolises the ground you walk on," she said. "You just want to be adored."

"This," said Laura with a grin, "is very true. Come on, we'd better go and do the handing-round-nibbles bit."

"The what? Laura, you didn't? You didn't let my mum talk you into that did you? I told her quite categorically that acting as unpaid waitresses just wasn't on."

Laura shrugged. "You get to eat more that way," she commented, and pushed open the door.

Another ricochet of giggles emanated from the restaurant, followed by a trilling voice. "Anona! How lovely to see you! Love the hair, darling— and Henry. Oh, I love a man with a powerful hug!"

Ginny Gee was clasping Henry Joseph to her somewhat capacious bosom and puckering her lips alarmingly.

Chelsea closed her eyes. "I don't believe it," she sighed. "She ought to be locked up."

"And Jon," shrilled Mrs. Gee, "don't look so lost, dear—Laura's in the loo prettying herself up for you. She won't be a tick."

Laura slammed the door shut again and stared at Chelsea. "Tell me she didn't say what I think she just said," she whispered.

Chelsea shook her head. "Don't blame me," she said firmly. "I told you she was a walking disaster area. Come on, you'd better get out there and rescue Jon. I'll just find a quiet corner in which to curl up and die."

It was quite amazing, thought Jon Joseph morosely, shuffling his feet in embarrassment, how someone only had to hand his parents a glass of wine and something nondescript on a stick for them to switch on the charm and look as if they were the most united couple on earth. No one watching his mother now, smiling and laughing with Laura's mum, or listening to his father holding forth, in his normal bombastic way, to Chelsea's dad about property prices, would believe that an hour before they had been shouting at one another so loudly that Jon had rushed round the house shutting windows, in case the Farrants next door heard the hurled abuse.

"You just don't try to understand, do you?" his mother had yelled, slamming her interior-design manuals down on the dining-room table and running her fingers distractedly through her newly highlighted blond hair. "For years, I've done what you wanted, supported *you* in *your* job—and now, just when I'm getting myself established doing what I want with my life, you come up with this harebrained idea and expect me to just drop everything and fit in with your plans. It simply isn't fair!"

"Oh, isn't it?" Jon's father had boomed, his already ruddy complexion deepening alarmingly. "But I suppose it's perfectly fair to expect me to carry on in a job I detest, working ridiculous hours in the company of young whiz kids who seem to think they know it all. It's all very well for you, dabbling in your college course . . ."

"I am not dabbling!"

"Well, you're not exactly busting a gut, are you?"

At which point, Jon had stormed into the dining-room and demanded to know what was going on. Of course, in typical parental fashion, his mother had assumed one of those too-bright, plastic smiles and told him not to worry his head, and his father had glared at him and said that it was a personal matter between the two of them and nothing to do with him. All the way to the restaurant Jon's parents had sat in stony silence, his father slamming the gears unnecessarily fiercely, and his mother sighing deeply every time he overtook another car. And now, hey presto! it was all sweetness and light, and lovely to see you and yes, thank you, we had a brilliant Christmas.

But it hadn't been brilliant. The only good part about it had been Boxing Day afternoon, when he had cycled round to Laura's house and given her his present—a really wicked book of cartoons by Blob. It had cost a bomb, but Blob was by far the most cutting political cartoonist around, and Laura was one of the few people who hadn't laughed when Jon told her that he wanted to follow in his footsteps. The trouble was that Laura hadn't seemed over the moon with the book and had only flicked through it before starting on the usual questions, like, "You do love me, don't you?" and "What do you feel when I kiss you?" Since what Jon felt when Laura kissed him wasn't something you could easily put into words, and he wasn't altogether sure that he should be feeling it, he had sort of shrugged and said, "I dunno," and then felt a complete nerd when she went all chilly on him. But tonight, he was going to do it properly, say all the right things and let her see how much he really loved her.

"You all right, dear?" His mother had drifted away from Mrs. Turnbull.

"Mmm," muttered Jon. "Mum, what was all that arguing about, back at the house?"

His mother waved a hand dismissively. "Oh, just your father having one of his stresses," she said.

"About what?"

"Oh, pressure of work, pointlessness of life, that sort of thing," said his mother, taking a sip of wine. "He gets like that every few months—he'll get over it."

"But I heard you say something about a plan . . ."

"Oh, Jon, it's not important," interrupted his mother impatiently. "And, anyway, you shouldn't have been listening."

"With the kind of noise you two were making, it would have been pretty hard not to," retorted Jon. "Things are all right between you, aren't they?"

"Yes," said his mother, rather too shortly and without a great deal of conviction. "Oh, there's Chitrita—I must go and have a word."

Jon chewed his lip. He hoped she was right. His father could be a complete pain at times, always trying to make out he knew more than he did, but ever since he had decided that he had to get fit, and Jon had taken him along to the gym in the hope that he would stop making an exhibition of himself by jogging round the streets in a purple and yellow shell suit, they had done the odd workout together and talked more. Although Jon couldn't say they agreed on much, at least they weren't permanently fighting.

He was about to cross over to quiz his father about this mysterious plan, when Laura appeared at his elbow. "Hi, Jon, have a—well, I think it's a prawn thing," she said, smiling up at him. As she thrust a tray of canapés under his nose, all thoughts of parental differences went out of his mind. She looked gorgeous. She smelt divine. He had to get it right this time.

You look lovely, he said silently in his head.

No, too naff.

Can't wait for later, he rehearsed.

No, too much of a come-on.

I think I'm in love with you, perhaps?

No, too slushy.

10

"I like prawns," he said.

"Oh good," said Laura tightly. "Oh—hi, Sumitha!"

And, snatching the tray from Jon's outstretched hand, she pushed across the room without a backward glance.

I've done it again, I've blown it, thought Jon miserably, glancing at his watch. Two more hours before the disco starts. Then I'll tell her. When I've got her to myself. By then, I'll have worked out what to say. After all, two hours won't make any difference.

One hour and fifty-five minutes to go till I see him, thought Sumitha Banerji, standing meekly beside her parents and wondering why it was that, when every other father in the room was dressed in casual shirts and chinos, her dad had to come to a party wearing a pin-striped suit and looking as if he was about to address a board meeting. Not that she should worry; the fact that her parents were at this party at all was the only thing that really mattered. There was no way her father, for whom chilling-out was an unknown concept, would have let her go to The Stomping Ground's New Year Stampede if it hadn't been for Mrs. Gee, who lived in the real world, assuring him that all the other parents were in favour and, anyway, what could happen when all of them were partying just across the road?

"This will be the very last party, Sumitha, until your examinations are over," he had intoned earlier, as they were driving to Gee Whiz. "You have much work to do if you are to achieve your true potential."

Rajiv Banerji had a tendency to speak like a school report.

"Her grades last term were very good, Rajiv dear," Sumitha's mother had offered tentatively.

"There was room for improvement," her father began. "At least two of those Bs should have been As."

"But what is the saying here—all work and no play makes James an unhappy boy?" queried Mrs. Banerji.

"Jack a dull boy!" Sumitha had laughed. She was laughing a lot lately. Not even the sight of her mother being typically unliberated and hanging on to her father's every word, or the battery of disapproving glances from her dad, as he eyed the ultra-tight black Lycra hipsters she had bought

12

surreptitiously in the sales, could stress her out. Because, in just under two hours, she would be at The Stomping Ground. Close to *him*.

She hadn't told anyone about Seb. Not yet. This time, she wasn't taking any chances. Because this time it really was special. Seb was utterly divine, with piercing ice-blue eyes, long, crinkly, fair hair and a lopsided grin which made her stomach turn somersaults in a very undisciplined manner. The fact that he was white, eighteen years old, and played in a band called Paper Turkey were three excellent reasons for not drawing her parents' attention to his existence. Besides which, a secret love was so romantic.

"You look pleased with yourself!" Laura appeared at her side, proffering a dish of roasted cashew nuts to her parents. "I suppose people who get the highest grades in the year yet again do have the right to the odd grin. Or do you have some dark and intimate secret?"

"Of course not!" snapped Sumitha, throwing her a warning glance as Rajiv's eyebrows shot heavenwards.

"Pity," said Laura. "Have a prawn."

Ginny Gee looked anxiously at her watch and then at the street door. The Farrants were late and Barry was getting all hot under the collar about the meal. He hadn't invited the local glitterati and top business people, only to have his *pièce de résistance* ruined by latecomers.

"I don't know whether to start or wait another five minutes," she murmured to Ruth Turnbull. "One doesn't want to look rude but then, on the other hand, if Barry's surprise gets spoiled, he'll be in a mood till Easter."

She glanced towards the kitchen door, where Barry was gesticulating furiously through the glass pane. "I suppose I could phone them," she said.

"Let me," interrupted Ruth hastily. "You go on being the perfect hostess. I'll do it."

She rushed across to the foyer and picked up the receiver on the pay phone. Glancing anxiously over her shoulder, she dialled a number.

"Jemma, will you just get into that car and stop making such a ridiculous fuss about nothing!" stormed Andrew Farrant, opening the back door of his Volvo and gesturing at her impatiently.

"Oh, so my entire future is nothing now, is it?" yelled Jemma, flicking her fringe out of her eyes. "Not content with ruining my Christmas, you want to mess up my whole life! Well, I'm not going to let you!"

Her father shoved her, none too gently, into the back seat, snapped, "Seat belt!" at her, and climbed in behind the wheel. Her mother, dressed in a rather extraordinary blue taffeta frock of uncertain age, was nibbling a fingernail and looking rather like someone waiting for root canal work. "Jemma petal . . ."

"Don't call me petal!"

"Sorry. Can't we just let the subject drop for now? Don't spoil the evening."

Jemma glared at her. "Oh, so it's all right for you to spoil my chances of ever being a professional actress, but I mustn't spoil your poxy night out, is that it? First you stop me being in the panto at The Royal, just because of a few stupid exams, and now you're saying I can't do the new advert. It's just not fair!"

Jemma sat seething in the car, while her father swore quietly at every passing motorist and tapped his fingers on the steering wheel at every red light.

"Can't you just let me . . ." she began in one last attempt.

"Jemma! Will you stop it right now!" stormed her father, swinging the car into the forecourt of Gee Whiz. "The subject is closed. All this drama stuff has gone far enough. Nothing is more important this year than your GCSEs—nothing at all. You have mock exams in just a few days' time and your end-of-term report was hardly inspiring . . ."

"Oh that's right, drag all that up again!"

". . . and you need decent grades to do your A levels, and . . ."

"How many times do I have to tell you? I'm not doing A levels! I'm going to drama school. In London. Next year."

"Over my dead body," said her father, snapping the steering lock on to the wheel and opening the door.

"That," muttered Jemma under her breath, "could be arranged."

"And you're absolutely sure, Margot, that it's just tiredness. I mean, he hasn't got a fever, or . . . okay. Well, hold him up to the phone so I can talk to him."

Ruth cupped her hand to the receiver and threw

another quick glance over her shoulder. "And is oo Mummy's good wickle boy, den? Is oo? Is Charlie going to stop cwying now and go to beddybyes for Auntie Margot?"

"MUM! What are you doing?"

Ruth wheeled round to find Laura, hands on hips, glaring at her.

"Chelsea's mum says don't bother phoning Mrs. Farrant, they've arrived," said her daughter. "It appears you weren't, anyway. You're wittering over Charlie again, aren't you? Honestly, Mum, you're neurotic."

"Sorry, Margot, must go—nighty-night, boofuls boy."

Ruth slammed down the receiver. "I just phoned to see if Charlie had settled—he's been so grizzly all day."

"He's probably fed up with being pawed over," snapped Laura. "You smother that child. If you're not very careful, you're going to end up like Jemma's mum."

"I was just . . ."

"And you've got to stop speaking to Charlie in baby talk."

Ruth gave an exasperated sigh. "Babies like

sing-song language, the musicality gives them con-fidence—my *Parenting for the Nineties* book said so. And besides, I used to talk to you like that, and you're not exactly lost for words."

"I," said Laura, "rose above it."

"Chelsea my sweet, do come and meet Trudie Lambert!" Chelsea's mother flung an arm round her shoulders.

"Mum!" hissed Chelsea from between clenched teeth, wriggling in the ever-tightening embrace.

Ginny took no notice. "Trudie, this is my darling Chelsea—Chelsea, meet Trudie, the new pro-gramme director at Radio L."

Why, thought Chelsea, shaking the proffered hand and grinning in a somewhat sickly manner, does my mother have to go into theatrical mode and pretend to be a doting parent whenever her colleagues are near? For someone who ignores my existence the rest of the time, it does seem rather hypocritical.

"Good to meet you, Chelsea," said Trudie, who appeared to have the entire contents of a Boots make-up department on her cheekbones. "I've heard a lot about you."

"My inspiration, aren't you, darling?" gushed her mother. "Trudie's awfully keen on pulling in the younger listener, aren't you, Trudie?"

Trudie inclined her head. "Indeed—a lot has to change if Radio Leehampton is to stop the rot," she said, still pumping Chelsea's hand.

Ginny flushed. "Yes, well, of course, you're so right—we have to cater to the young because they are the listening audience of tomorrow and, I have to say, you couldn't find anyone on the station who has been more vocal than myself in encouraging a younger, fresher outlook. Isn't that right, Chelsea dear?"

Chelsea nodded, because that was obviously what she was supposed to do, although in truth she hadn't a clue what her mother was on about. Not that there was anything new about that.

"Oh yes indeedy," babbled Ginny. "A young outlook, that's what we all want."

She paused, suddenly appreciating just what she had said. "In content, that is," she added hastily. "There's no substitute for the mature, experienced broadcaster."

"Oh, I don't know that I agree," said Trudie, finally releasing Chelsea's hand and taking a sip of wine. "I am all for bringing in fresh voices, fresh talent. In any case, you'll hear my ideas soon enough, at next week's restructuring meeting."

Ginny bit her lip. "Restructuring?"

Trudie nodded.

"Oh. Yes," murmured Ginny, flushing slightly and fixing an even brighter grin on her face. "Well, yes of course I'll do any slot—morning, late night, Sunday—you know me, I'll fit in with anything."

Chelsea shifted her weight and edged away.

"Yes well, let's leave it for now, shall we?" smiled Trudie. "No point mixing business with pleasure."

"Oh, but my work is my pleasure!" Ginny assured her.

"Oh puke," said Chelsea.

"Pardon?" said Trudie.

"Happy New Year," said Chelsea, who was wondering why on earth her mother should be so keen to talk business at what was supposed to be a madly happy party.

Especially when it made her look as if she was attending a wake.

"You look nice." Jon rushed out the words and stared at the floorboards with intent concentration.

Sumitha looked surprised. "Oh—thank you," she said, thinking how amazing it was that, only a few months before, she had really fancied Jon. But that, of course, had been when she was a mere adolescent, with unformed emotions and misguided ambitions.

"Youlookprettyinthosetrouserthings," he gabbled, rather pleased with himself for having the brilliant idea of practising his chat-up lines on someone whose reaction didn't matter. "New?"

Sumitha's eyes widened in puzzlement.

"Er—yes," she said. This was worrying. Jon had hardly spoken to her in six months, and suddenly he was making in-depth enquiries about her wardrobe. She did hope he wasn't falling for her again because she would have to tell him, very gently of course, that she simply wasn't available.

"It's hot in here, isn't it?" said Jon, who had thought that his black polo neck and slate leather jacket would be mega cool but now felt rather like a toasted tea-cake.

Oh no, thought Sumitha. That's the oldest line in the book. It comes just before, "Shall we go out and get some air for a bit?" What's with him? she wondered. He and Laura are supposed to be an item, for heaven's sake. More important, how do I get rid of him?

She was about to make some feeble excuse about needing the loo, when there was a scraping of chairs and general commotion on the far side of the restaurant.

"Oh look," she said brightly. "It looks like we're about to eat."

Chelsea's mum was climbing on to a chair.

"Or something," she added.

"Oh no, what's she doing now?" Chelsea grabbed Jemma's arm and closed her eyes in horror.

Her mother was standing on the chair, clapping her hands and gesticulating at everyone to be quiet. Her exceedingly tight and somewhat short black-berry velvet mini-skirt had ridden up, exposing large quantities of fishnet-clad thighs and a glimpse of lace knicker, a fact which appeared not to bother her in the slightest, but made Chelsea want the ground to open and swallow her up.

"Barry and I are thrilled to pieces that you could all come along tonight," Ginny declared. "Old friends and new . . ." She threw a sparkling grin at Trudie. ". . . Young and old—such fun!"

Shut up, Mum. Please, just shut up.

"Now, do please take your places at the tables, because Barry has a little surprise for you all."

There was a murmur of anticipation as couples began shuffling towards their seats.

"You children—sorry, young people." Ginny gave a high-pitched giggle and Chelsea felt like throwing up into the nearest pot plant. "You young people are all together at the window table, so you can have fun away from us oldies." She beamed in acknowledgement of her status as a totally understanding parent.

"And now," exclaimed Ginny, gesturing towards the kitchen door, "the Surprise! Ta-ra!!"

She flung her arms wide open and her silk shirt stretched alarmingly over her not-inconsiderable chest. The door opened and everyone gasped. A Scots piper marched slowly into the room, followed by a lanky, fair-haired boy carrying a silver salver, on which was what looked like a rather muddy Rugby ball. Behind him came Barry, grinning from ear to ear and brandishing a large knife.

"What's he doing here?" exclaimed Jon, above the wailing of the pipes.

"He's my father, actually," said Chelsea shortly. "He owns the place."

     23

"Not him, silly," said Jon. "Simon Stagg—the guy with the plate."

"Oh him," said Chelsea. "Work experience. He wants to be a chef."

Jon nodded. "That figures," he said. "He was the only one on the Duke of Edinburgh weekend who managed to cook a three-course meal over a gas stove."

"He's in your year, isn't he? Are you mates?"

"Not really," said Jon. "He's a bit wet."

The little procession had circled the room and stopped by the serving table.

"Oh I see—a haggis! Oh bravo, jolly good show!" a voice boomed above the pipes. Henry Joseph began clapping vigorously.

Shut up, Dad, thought Jon, glancing at Laura in embarrassment. Fortunately, Laura was staring open-mouthed at the proceedings and made no reaction.

"Did he say haggis?" murmured Jemma in Chelsea's left ear. "Please tell me he didn't say haggis."

"What is that thing?" asked Sumitha, as the piper stopped playing and everyone burst into applause.

"You really want to know?" asked Jemma.

Sumitha nodded.

"You don't want to know," Chelsea assured her. "Believe me, you don't want to know. And I promise, I didn't have any idea about this."

"Such an experience!" Chitrita Banerji exclaimed. "To taste this famous dish! Is it not exciting, Rajiv?"

Sumitha noted that her father had turned rather pale and was averting his eyes from Barry, who was standing, knife poised, at the table.

"So what is it?" she persisted, nudging Chelsea.

"It is," interrupted Jemma with disgust, "sheep's stomach filled with intestines."

"It is WHAT?" gasped Sumitha.

"You can't be serious?" murmured Jon. "Can you?"

Chelsea nodded. "Afraid so," she said. "Oh no, what now?"

Her dad had produced a sheet of paper and was beginning to read. "As you know, everyone, it is the custom to address the haggis before serving it . . ."

"He has definitely flipped," sighed Chelsea. "Is insanity catching?"

". . . and, therefore, I shall read Robert Burns's

seasonal poem before asking you to join me in our festive meal."

He began reading in an accent that wavered from bad Scottish to drunken Cornish and back to a sort of Geordie with Brummie overtones.

"Lovely, Barry dear!" interrupted Ginny at the end of the second verse, observing the astonished expressions on the faces of her guests, and whipping the sheet of paper from her husband's hands.

"I haven't finished," protested Barry.

"Yes, you have," asserted his wife.

Laura tapped Chelsea on the arm.

"Who is that?" Laura nodded towards Simon, who was handing round plates of haggis.

"Oh, some guy doing work experience with Dad," said Chelsea dismissively. "He's in Jon's year apparently."

Laura's eyes widened. "At Lee Hill? I've never seen him," she said. "How come I've never seen him before?"

Chelsea shrugged. "Considering there are over two hundred kids in that year, and considering you've spent the last heaven knows how long with your nose buried in Jon's chest, it's hardly surprising."

Laura sighed. "He's to die for," she breathed. "He looks like Keats."

"Who?"

"Your ignorance," sighed Laura, "is stultifying."

Simon came up to their table with a tray of plates.

"Haggis everyone?"

"No thanks," chorused Chelsea, Jemma, Jon, and Sumitha hastily.

"Great!" smiled Laura from underneath her eyelashes. "It looks wonderful."

"So do you!" smiled Simon, putting a plate in front of her.

Jon started, and spilt cola down his sweater. That should have been his line. Who did he think he was?

"Thanks," said Laura, inclining her head to one side and letting her tongue rest lightly on her lower lip.

"Enjoy your haggis—it was my idea to serve it and I'm not altogether sure it was a good one!"

"Oh it was!" enthused Laura. "I love—what did you say it was?"

"Haggis," repeated Simon. "It's traditional on New Year's Eve in Scotland. Must dash—I'm supposed to be making a sauce for the venison. The whole evening has a Scottish theme."

Jemma sighed. "Thank heavens I live in England," she said.

"This has gone on long enough," said Chelsea decisively, pushing back her chair and tossing her napkin on to the table. "Come on—let's go."

"Yes, do let's!" said Sumitha eagerly, jumping to her feet. "We don't want to be late."

"Great idea!" agreed Jon, who had failed miserably to get Laura to talk in anything but monosyllables and was hoping that the dim lighting and throbbing music of The Stomping Ground might focus her attention rather more. "Ready, Laura?" He threw her a glance which he hoped was full of unspoken promise.

Laura glanced at her watch. "But the disco doesn't start till nine," she protested, "and it's only ten to—it's dire getting there before everything's hotted up. Besides," she added, spooning up the last of her sauce, "we haven't had pudding yet."

"If the first two courses were anything to go by, we're not about to miss much," commented Chelsea.

At that moment Simon appeared with a large glass bowl.

"Pudding?" He touched Laura's shoulder and offered her a dish of something that looked like soggy polystyrene with bits in.

"What," asked Jon, peering into the dish with distaste, "is that?"

"Atholl Brose," said Simon.

"Excuse me?" said Laura.

"Cream, almonds, oatmeal . . ."

Laura wrinkled her nose. "Well . . ."

"It's okay," laughed Simon. "I'll let you off. Do you want me to look in the kitchen and see if there's any fruit salad left?"

"No, she doesn't!" interjected Jon, putting a firm hand on Laura's shoulder and propelling her towards the door. "We're just off. Aren't we, Laura?"

"Mmm," said Laura. And wondered why it was that, right now, staying here with a bowl of fruit salad seemed so much more attractive.

Love Lines

"I would have thought," began Rajiv Banerji, watching his daughter disappear through the door, "that you would have exercised some control over Sumitha's clothing."

His wife sighed. She was well used to her husband's conservative opinions about the raising of the young, but lately he had been even more dogmatic than ever, wanting Sumitha to wear *salwar kameez*, and even talking about contacting the Sheffield cousins in the hope of finding a suitable husband for her.

"But she's only fifteen!" Chitrita had gasped, when he had raised the subject yet again the previous day. "And, besides, we agreed—she marries for love. Arranged marriages . . ."

"Arranged marriages," Rajiv had replied, "have much going for them. Like marrying like, the compatibility of backgrounds."

"Love has a lot going for it too," Chitrita had murmured.

"Well, of course, and I would never force her to marry someone she did not think she could come to love and respect. But it is no bad thing to think ahead—after all, our parents planned for us to marry when you were only twelve, did they not?"

Chitrita had nodded.

"And has it been so very bad?" asked Rajiv more gently.

She had squeezed his hand. "Of course not," she had assured him. "It has been very good."

And it had. But, still—there were days when Chitrita still wondered what it would have been like to have a whole string of boyfriends, to experiment with different styles of dress, to actually be a teenager instead of a bride-in-waiting.

"Rajiv dear," she said, "just be thankful that Sumitha is as she is. She is a good girl; she works hard, she is not rebellious. Think how much worse things could be."

Rajiv nodded slowly. "At least," he said, spooning dessert into his mouth, "she has got over that boy-mad phase and come to her senses. We won't have that to contend with anymore."

Chitrita smiled. If that's what he wanted to think, then let him. It made for a far more peaceful life.

He wasn't there. But he had to be there. It said so on the poster outside the door: NEW YEAR STAMPEDE—WITH NEW LOCAL BAND, PAPER TURKEY. And, anyway, he had told her so himself, said that it was the band's first proper gig, apart from school ones, which didn't carry any real cred. And he had looked at her with those amazing, pale blue eyes and said, "You'd better be there!" as though it really mattered to him.

If it hadn't been for her father's remarkable lack of tolerance, Sumitha would never have bumped into Seb. It had been the day after the end of term, and her parents had invited some of their friends for a meal. Her father always went overboard on these occasions, making Sumitha and Sandeep tidy their bedrooms until they were as spotless as operating theatres waiting for open-heart surgery to be performed, even though none of the guests would set foot upstairs. And then, just an hour before the first guest was due to arrive, he had looked out of the sitting-room window.

"My goodness me, what it that?" he exclaimed with such alarm that his wife abandoned the *badami murghi* that she was making and came rushing into the room.

"It's a van, dear," she commented.

"But it is parked across my driveway!" expostulated Rajiv, turning towards the door.

"Our driveway," corrected Chitrita. "And no need to make a fuss, Rajiv, I am sure it will be moved in a moment."

Sumitha, who had heard the exclamations while she was varnishing her toenails a rather fetching shade of Sunburst Gold, hopped into the room, her toes held apart with foam separators.

"What's going on?" she had asked.

"Well, you may ask!" stormed her father, who by now was pacing up and down in front of the window, a very definite warning sign of worse to come.

"Just look!" He had gesticulated out of the window.

Pulling up behind the van was a banana-yellow roadster of uncertain age, from which emanated the latest rap version of "Spot on Celia" at ear-blasting volume.

"This is too much!" Rajiv had shouted, turning

and heading for the door. "We moved here because it is supposed to be a good neighbourhood. I shall deal with it once and for all."

"Dad, wait!" Sumitha had pleaded, looking at her mother for support. Her dad was charming when things were going his way, but he was prone to say things in the heat of the moment which he—and his long-suffering family—regretted later. He had already complained to the Howletts next door that their honeysuckle had had the audacity to grow through their fence, and told the Rookes at number eighteen that their spaniel barked too loudly.

"It is no good saying that people like us suffer from racial intolerance if you then go shouting the odds at people without hearing them out," added Sumitha, removing the toe separators and slipping her feet carefully into her shoes.

Her father paused for just an instant, but it was long enough for her to dash to the front door. "I'll go and explain that we have guests arriving and ask them to move the cars—okay?" she said.

"Well, I . . ."

"Excellent idea, Sumitha," said her mother, with a sigh of relief. "Be polite, dear. Should I come too?"

"Yes," said Sumitha and opened the front door.

Climbing from the driving seat of the car, long blond hair flopping over sun-tanned cheeks, was the most mind-shattering guy ever.

"On second thought," said Sumitha. "No."

Standing now at the edge of the dance floor, trying to adjust her eyes to the dim lights and not look as if she was looking for anyone, Sumitha scanned The Stomping Ground. The nightclub was on two levels, and huge, overhead TV screens let you see what was going on upstairs while you were on the ground floor. But there was no sign of him. And he wasn't easy to miss—he was six feet tall and had this wonderful gravelly voice with just the hint of an accent she couldn't place. On the afternoon of the party, as she sped down the driveway in order to stop her father making a complete exhibition of himself, it had been his voice that had stopped her in her tracks.

"Hi there!" he had called, brushing a stray tendril of hair from his eyes and grinning at her. "Are you with our lot? I do rather hope so."

Sumitha had slowed to what she hoped was an elegant walk and opened her mouth. A small squeak came out.

"Er."

"Brill. I'm Seb. Seb Gundersen. And you are . . . ?"

"Sumitha Banerji. But actually . . ."

"Lovely name, really lyrical. Can you just help me with these drums?" he had said, gesturing to the back of the car, which was stacked high with instruments.

"Well, the thing is, I . . ."

He tipped the driving seat forward and leaned into the car. His black Levis tightened over his firm bottom.

"Yes, of course," said Sumitha, whose heart rate had doubled in the past sixty seconds and whose eyes seemed fixed on Seb's upper thigh area.

She had glanced back at the house, where her father was standing ramrod stiff, banging on the window with a clenched fist.

"Look," she had said hurriedly, "the thing is, my father's in a right strop because you are blocking our driveway. I don't suppose you could move up a bit? I mean, I know he's a right drag and . . ."

Seb had stood up in surprise. "This isn't Tate Reilly's place?" He had frowned, causing his nose to turn up ever so sexily.

Sumitha had shaken her head and pointed down

the road. "They live five doors down—The Poplars," she had said.

Seb had slapped his thigh in irritation. "Wrong house, Ross!" he shouted to the driver of the van, who leaned out of the door, chewing gum and looking impatient. "Five houses down."

The van door slammed and the vehicle edged forward along the kerb. From the window, Mr. Banerji nodded his approval and moved away.

"I knew it was trees of some sort," Seb said. "When I saw The Hollies on your gate, I guessed it must be this one. The gang usually practises at college, but during the holidays we have to find somewhere else—and my parents' tolerance level is incredibly low."

"Tell me about it," muttered Sumitha.

"So—you're not with us?"

Sumitha shook her head. "Who's us?" she had ventured, as he pushed a small drum back into the car and slammed the driving seat back into position.

"Paper Turkey," said Seb proudly. "About to become the greatest music sensation in the Western world. Well, in the East Midlands, anyway," he added with a throaty chuckle.

"Cool," said Sumitha. "What do you play?"

"Almost anything," he said. "It's kind of cool, poppy stuff with a few funky rap bits that Tate writes." He sat down and turned on the ignition. The car coughed reluctantly into life.

"Hey, listen," Seb said, as he jammed the car into gear, "we've got our first proper gig on New Year's Eve. At The Stomping Ground. You know it?"

Sumitha nodded eagerly.

"Great," Seb said. "So come along, why don't you? Bring your mates. We're not bad."

"I'll try," said Sumitha, deciding on the spot that if it meant tying her father up and locking him in the loo, she was going to get to the gig.

"You'd better be there!" he grinned, turning the car away from the kerb. "See you, Sumitha!"

And with a wave, he'd disappeared round the bend. And he'd got her name right. Most non-Indian guys either called her Sumatra or Suminder, or simply gave up and called her Sue, which drove her crazy. But Seb had got it right first time.

Her thoughts were jolted back to the present by a voice in her left ear.

"Sumitha, what are you doing?" Chelsea nudged

her arm. "You've been standing there for the last five minutes, like some lost soul. We've grabbed a table by the stage—we thought we could eye up the talent."

"I'll be over in just a minute," said Sumitha. And if there's eyeing up to be done, she thought, I'm having first refusal.

Street Cred For Sumitha

"**H**ey, Jemma, you look mizz—are you missing Rob?" asked Laura, tapping her feet to the disco beat and wishing Jon would stop yacking to his mates and ask her to dance. "When does he get back from skiing?"

"Tomorrow," muttered Jemma.

"So that's why you look so murderous!" teased Chelsea, slumping back down in her seat. "I wouldn't worry, that guy over there in the black army pants is giving you the eye. Play your cards right and I reckon you're in there!"

"Some of us have more important things to think about than pulling the nearest thing in trousers!" retorted Jemma, picking up her blackcurrant and cola and glaring at Chelsea.

"Sorr-eee!" replied Chelsea, holding up her hands in mock surrender.

Jemma sighed. "Sorry, I didn't mean to snap," she said. "I am just so angry right now I could explode."

"What's wrong?" asked Laura.

"Parents!" spat Jemma. "You just would not believe the way they've been these last few weeks. Just because of these stupid mocks . . ."

"Oh don't!" groaned Chelsea. "Have you had the If-you- spent-as-much-time-studying-as-you-spend-on-the-telephone-you-might-get-somewhere-in-life bit?"

"And the bit about it being time you joined the real world?" volunteered Laura.

Jemma raised her eyes to the ceiling. "And the rest!" she said. "It's constant nag, nag, nag. Even tonight, they couldn't let it go—they just went on and on about how I have to do well in my GCSEs in order to be able to stay on for A levels."

Laura frowned. "But you said you didn't want to do As," she pointed out. "You said you were going to drama school."

"Precisely!" said Jemma emphatically. "You know that, I know that. The parents, however, seem unable to grasp that simple fact. It's not even as though there's any logic to them; first they're holding forth about jobs being hard to come by and what you put in you get out, and all that stuff, and then, when I get the chance to be in this TV advert, they say I can't take time off from studying. Bizarre or what?"

"Unreal," agreed Chelsea. "I reckon rational thought escapes them after the age of forty. Mine are just as chronic. Hey, look, he's coming this way!"

She nudged Jemma.

"He's a pretty fit guy, don't you reckon?"

"Not my type," murmured Jemma, uncrossing her legs and tugging at her skirt.

"Oh good," said Chelsea. "Then I'll have him."

"Have who?" said Sumitha, pushing past a crowd of girls who were sitting on the edge of the stage, and dumping her drink on the table.

"The lush guy with the legs," said Chelsea, jerking her head in his direction, while closely examining her fingernails, in case he was looking. It didn't do to look too eager. He really was rather gorgeous. Tall, rangy, with a mass of undisciplined fair hair flopping over his left eye. His face was pulled into a worried frown and, for some reason, Chelsea had a sudden image of his sun-tanned face resting on her shoulder while she soothed his worried brow.

"It's him!"

Chelsea's rather evocative imaginings were rudely interrupted by Sumitha, who had leaped out of her chair, pushed past her—spilling drink all over the table as she did so—and sauntered up to the fair guy, fluffing up her hair and smiling coyly.

"Hi, Seb!"

"Watch it!" muttered Chelsea, swinging her knees round to avoid the steady stream of cola that was heading for her lap.

Sumitha couldn't believe she was doing this. She would never normally go up to someone she hardly knew and start up a conversation. What if he didn't remember her? Or, worse still, ignored her? It would be so embarrassing. But once Chelsea got her claws into him, she wouldn't stand a chance.

"Hi, Seb, how's it going?" she repeated, raising her voice above the noise of the music and hoping she sounded more confident than she felt.

"What . . . oh it's Sumitha, isn't it? Hi!"

Chelsea gasped as the tall guy broke into a broad grin and gave Sumitha a friendly punch on the shoulder. "You came—ace!"

His eyes travelled from her sleek black bob, down her slim figure, and back again.

"You look great," he said. "Come round the back, why don't you, and meet the guys? We're on in twenty minutes but there's just time. You might calm our nerves."

"Cool," said Sumitha, noting with intense pleasure the looks of sheer amazement on the faces of her friends.

"Who," breathed Laura, "was that?"

"Whoever he was," said Chelsea with a sigh, "it appears Sumitha has got him. Life can be very unjust."

Right, thought Jon, gulping down some apple fizz and taking a deep breath. This is it.

"Let's dance," he said to Laura.

"Okay," said Laura, with rather less enthusiasm than he would have liked.

They made it look so easy on TV, he thought, beginning to move with the music. You looked in the girl's eyes and said something cool and she melted into your arms and then you kissed. Well, it had to be fairly easy, otherwise they wouldn't do it in the soaps. That was supposed to be real life, after all.

He swallowed and gazed into Laura's face with what he hoped was a loving yet commanding look. Unfortunately, her eyes were closed. Or was that good? Perhaps that meant she was transported with passion, just being with him.

He glanced at one of the overhead screens which showed a couple in a dead-close clinch. The guy was running his hands down the girl's back.

Good idea, thought Jon. He edged closer and put his arms round her neck. Her eyes were still closed and there was a faint smile spreading over her rather luscious lips. He ran his hands down her back. She smiled more broadly and sighed a little. This was working. He was getting it right.

"You smell lovely," he whispered, brushing his lips across her left earlobe.

"Mm?" murmured Laura.

"This is nice, isn't it?" he said, and then wished he hadn't because it didn't sound even halfway cool. "I mean, being close, it's—well, it's—you know, isn't it?"

Laura gave a half nod.

He wished she would open her eyes. He wanted to kiss her, but her head was in the wrong place.

"Look at me," he said, trying to make his voice sound throaty.

I don't want to look at you, thought Laura, keeping her eyes tightly shut. I want to carry on just like this.

The track was coming to an end. Time was running out.

"Laura, look at me," he said in desperation. "Please."

Very slowly, and very reluctantly, Laura opened her eyes. Jon leaned forward, took a deep breath and kissed her. She wished she'd kept her eyes closed. That way, it was so much easier to pretend it was Simon's arms that were holding her.

"Should I just give another ring, do you think?"

Ruth chewed her bottom lip and eyed the clock anxiously. "He gets so fretful when he's teething and . . ."

"Oh, for goodness sake, Ruth!" Melvyn shouted, and then lowered his voice when he caught sight of Claire Farrant's disapproving stare. "Charlie will be fine with Margot—she's had four kids of her own."

"I know, I know, but she can be very offhand about things and . . ."

"She's not offhand, she's just not neurotic like you," said Melvyn, and instantly regretted the remark when he saw Ruth's crestfallen expression.

"I'm sorry, love, but it's been ages since you and I have had an evening out on our own, and it would be nice if we could just talk about something other than Charlie for a while."

"What's that about Charlie?" gushed Ginny Gee, rushing up with a bottle of wine and refilling their glasses. "How is the adorable little pumpkin?"

"Well, he's a bit off today," said Ruth. "But, do you know, yesterday he actually managed to . . ."

"Excuse me," said Melvyn through gritted teeth, pushing back his chair and standing up.

He strode over to the neighbouring table where Barry Gee and Henry Joseph were sharing a joke. "Barry," said Melvyn, "do you find the subject of cutting teeth tremendously gripping?"

"No," said Barry, looking puzzled.

"Henry," said Melvyn, "do you want to spend the next twenty minutes discussing the relative merits of four different brands of toddler food?"

"Certainly not," said Henry.

"Good," said Melvyn. "In that case, may I join you?"

There is nothing more embarrassing, thought Chelsea, sipping a lemonade and trying to look disinterested in life, than sitting on your own when all your mates are dancing and gossiping.

She and Jemma had given it a go on the floor for a while but then Grant Nisbet from school had sidled up to Jemma and she had disappeared into the crowd with him. Admittedly, Warren Timbrell had sort of shaken himself up and down in front of her for a while, but every time he punched the air, in what he obviously thought was a very hip manner, it became very apparent that he was not into using deodorant and, since stringing sentences together didn't appear to be his forte either, she had beat a hasty retreat at the first opportunity.

She was just about to give up and shut herself in the loo when she saw a familiar figure waving frantically and shoving her way through the dancers to reach her.

"Hi, Chelsea! Haven't seen you in ages! How's life?"

A tall girl, with bleached blond hair cut in a short crop, enveloped her in a hug. She was wearing thick gold lipstick, and the sandy-coloured eye make-up couldn't disguise the dark rings under her eyes.

"Wha . . . Bex? It is you! Wow, you look different."

The last time Chelsea had seen her, Bex Bayliss had had raven-black hair cut into hedgehog spikes, and a lot of attitude. Bex was a year older than Chelsea and when she was at Lee Hill, she had been known as the school rebel. During what Chelsea's father called her "bad patch" and Chelsea remembered as the three most miserable months of her life so far, she had got pretty matey with Bex and her gang, and bunked off school and been, she had to admit, pretty stupid. But when one of the guys in the gang had come on too strong to Chelsea one night and scared the life out of her, it had been Bex who had chased after her, comforted her and made her see that her life was, by and large, pretty okay. Bex had left Lee Hill after failing her GCSEs and Chelsea hadn't seen her in months.

"Come on, sit down," said Chelsea, delighted to have someone to talk to.

"It's so cool to see you again," beamed Bex, slumping on to the chair. "So, what's the goss? You still at school? GCSEs?"

"Worse luck," said Chelsea, fixing as bored an expression on her face as she could manage.

"Well, at least you're not likely to mess up like I did," said Bex, fiddling with a copper earring. "Was I one idiot! I only got English and art, and I've had to retake loads. Still, I've got them now."

Chelsea stared at her in surprise. Bex had always seemed the type of girl who couldn't care less about qualifications and things.

"I'm living in London now—and guess what? I'm doing beauty therapy."

"Neat!" said Chelsea in admiration. "So how come you've ditched the bright lights for this dead hole?" She drummed her fingers on the table and tried to look as if a night at The Stomping Ground was the pits.

Bex sighed. "I came home for Christmas, and Ricky—that's my kid brother—well, he really got me worried. So I came back this weekend to check him out."

She nibbled a highly varnished fingernail.

"What do you mean?" asked Chelsea.

Bex tossed her head. "Oh, nothing—I'm probably overreacting. It's just—well . . ."

"Yes?"

"My mum knocks him about a bit. I mean, she did it to me, but I could look after myself. Ricky's different—really timid and pretty much a loner."

Chelsea swallowed. What could she say? How could anyone get hit by their own mother? It was awful.

"Anyway," said Bex, over-brightly, "how's life with you?"

"Life? What life?" asked Chelsea, grateful for an excuse to change the subject. "School, work, revision, exams, being nagged for low grades, more school, work, revision . . . and so on and so on."

"Oh well, only two more terms," said Bex. "Then freedom!"

Chelsea frowned. "Two and half years, more like," she said.

"Only if you want to," reasoned Bex. "You don't have to stay on."

"Well, no—but I mean, everyone does."

"I didn't. No one can make you, not once you're sixteen. There is a world beyond Leehampton, Chelsea—and believe me, it's a lot more exciting than school. I've got it made—two days a week in college, four days at the salon—and a social life to die for!"

She sipped her drink and yawned. "So what's with this new band everyone's going on about then?" she asked brightly. " 'Course, down in London I go to loads of gigs—this lot will probably be mega drear."

Probably, thought Chelsea. Pretty much like everything else in Leehampton.

"Okay, guys, one more track and you're on."

The disco manager slapped Seb on the back and turned to Sumitha, who was gazing at the way Seb's hair curled round his shoulders. "Are you the lead singer?"

Sumitha stared at him. "Me? Oh no, no—I'm nothing to do with it, I'm just . . ."

"She's with me," interrupted Seb, so decisively that Sumitha's legs turned immediately to the consistency of jelly.

"Prettiest roadie I've seen in a long time!" grinned the manager, glancing once more at his watch. "Good luck, guys—sock it to them!"

"My mouth's gone all dry," complained Tate, who was the smallest, billed as the Teeny Tunesmith, and looked more like a sixteen-year-old than a guy in his fresher year at uni.

"Oh man, am I scared!" groaned Ross, clasping one hand to his head and grabbing his guitar with the other.

As the sounds of "Animal Incorporated" faded, and the DJ mopped his brow, the disco manager strode on stage.

"Good luck!" whispered Sumitha.

"Thanks," murmured Seb. "I'll catch you later—you can tell me what you think."

I think, thought Sumitha, running down the side steps of the stage and back to their table, that you are the most gorgeous, to-die-for guy I have ever met. I think that if I can't see you again, I shall most probably die. I think this is the happiest day of my entire life.

She flopped on to her seat with a sigh. The others were already leaning forward, eagerly waiting for the band to come on stage.

"And now, for the very first time at The Stomping Ground, three local boys with sounds as catchy as a summer cold. They're cool, they're poppy and they're home-brewed—they're Paper Turkey!"

To a burst of enthusiastic applause, the band came on stage and struck up their first number.

ⓖ   ✿   ⓖ   ✿   ⊚   ✿   ⊚   **53**

"That's the guy you were chatting up!" gasped Chelsea to Sumitha as Seb executed a flourishing drum-roll.

"Yes," said Sumitha. "I know him."

"You know him?" queried Chelsea, as if Sumitha had just acknowledged an intimate acquaintance with the prime minister. "How come?"

"We met," said Sumitha enigmatically.

The tempo quickened and the volume increased. "They're good," said Bex approvingly, after a few minutes.

"I know," said Sumitha, as proudly as if she had personally groomed them for stardom.

"That guy on the drums is sensational," muttered Jon.

"That's Seb," said Sumitha smugly.

"Couldn't you just eat that dreamy guy on the bass guitar?" asked Jemma.

"That's Tate," Sumitha informed her.

"He is so cute," breathed Jemma, edging her chair nearer to the stage. "Do you actually know all these guys?"

"Oh yes," said Sumitha airily. "Ever so well."

Plan A

Laura glanced up at the clock above the bar. Eleven P.M. If she didn't do it soon, it would be too late. Of course, she shouldn't really be thinking about him at all, not while Jon had his arms firmly entwined round her neck and was telling her how cute she was. She had tried to put him out of her mind, to concentrate on summoning up that squidgy, smoochy feeling that kissing Jon used to create, but it didn't work. As her fingers fiddled idly with a strand of Jon's curly hair, she kept imagining what it would feel like to have Simon's cheek pressed against hers.

"It's really hot, isn't it?" she said to Jon, brushing a hand across her forehead. "Mind if I sit down for a bit?"

"No, sure—do you want a drink or something?"

Laura nodded and then shook her head. If he got her a drink, he would stand at the bar, and she had to walk that way to reach the door.

"No, I'll be fine—say, why don't you ask Chelsea to dance? She's been a bit out of things this evening."

Jon nodded. "Okay," he said. "You know, you really are a kind-hearted person, aren't you?"

Laura stifled a pang of guilt.

"Just as long as the rest of the night we're together?" pressed Jon.

Laura squashed another, rather larger pang of guilt. "Mmmm" she said. And wondered just what she would do if the first part of her scheme actually worked.

"And there you have them—Paper Turkey! I guess those guys are heading for the big time! Just remember, you heard them first here at the great SG!"

The manager had jumped on to the stage and was enthusiastically adding to the applause, foot stamping, and whistles from the dance floor.

Seb, Tate, and Ross gave a final air-punch and Tate and Ross waved their guitars in the air. As the cheers got louder, they ran to the side of the stage and jumped down into the audience.

"Oh my gosh! They're coming this way! I can't

look!" Jemma dug Sumitha in the ribs. "Is he looking?"

"Is who looking?" frowned Sumitha jealously.

"The gorgeous one—that Tate guy, the one that sang," persisted Jemma. "Don't look!"

"Jemma," said Sumitha with mock patience, "if I don't look, I can't see if he's looking at you not looking."

"And now," cried the manager, "here's our resident DJ, Spike Shayler, to take us all up to midnight when the band will be back to play in the new year!"

As the DJ played the first track, the guys grabbed glasses from a side table and took long gulps of shandy. A crowd of kids began pressing round them, and a flame-haired man, wearing a lime-green shirt and blue jacket, grabbed Tate by the arm and began talking earnestly, waving his arms in the air and pulling sheets of paper from his inside pocket.

"He is so cute!" breathed Jemma, her eyes fixed on Tate's baby face.

"Want to dance, Chelsea?" asked Jon.

"Why not?" said Chelsea, who was getting a bit sick of all this outpouring of adoration. Particularly as she had no one handy to adore.

"You know them," Jemma said eagerly to Sumitha. "You go and talk to them and I'll kind of tag along behind."

"Okay," said Sumitha, proud to be the one in the know. They shouldered their way through the throng to where Seb, Tate, and Ross were standing, looking slightly shellshocked and clutching sheets of paper.

The man in the blue jacket was beginning to edge away. "So remember, guys," Sumitha heard him say, "it's up to you. You can go for it or funk out—but you have to make your mind up pretty quick. Got it?"

"Got it!" chorused the band, looking like three kids who've discovered that Santa Claus has been in April.

"You were brilliant," whispered Jemma. No one appeared to hear.

"Go for what?" asked Sumitha.

Seb shook his head slowly in amazement. "The Battle of the Bands," he said.

"The what?"

"It's this huge gig festival for new bands—real prestige stuff. We sent off a demo tape ages ago, just for a laugh really, and that guy was one of the scouts. He reckons we're in for the East Midlands regional heat."

"Only, he said we needed to be more gimmicky on stage," added Ross.

"So we get gimmicky," said Tate decisively.

Ross didn't look convinced.

"It can really open doors," added Seb enthusiastically, raising his voice above the sounds of the latest rap hit. "Recording contracts, warm-up slots with top names—the works."

"But you have to be something special to get anywhere," said Ross.

"You are," insisted Sumitha. "Really special."

"Do you really think so?" asked Tate, his forehead puckering anxiously.

"Think so? You're the best sound around," she said, hoping the phrase made her sound knowledgeable about the music scene. "Aren't they, Jemma?"

She gave her friend a nudge. Jemma was standing, mouth half open, gazing at Tate.

"This is Jemma," said Sumitha. "Believe it or not, there are times when she manages to string a few words together."

Jemma threw her a glare, opened her mouth and shut it again.

"So, are we up for it?" asked Seb.

"You bet!" affirmed Tate.

"Okay, you guys," said Seb decisively. "Let's grab another beer and do some serious brainstorming. Catch you after midnight, girls!"

"We have to go on the dot of midnight—our parents . . ." began Jemma, and stopped abruptly as Sumitha's black patent clog addressed her big toe.

"No sweat," shrugged Seb, as the three drifted off to a corner table without a backward glance.

"That," said Sumitha, "was about the most uncool thing I have ever heard you say. You make it sound as if our whole lives are governed by what our parents say."

"Sadly," said Jemma, "they are."

Revelations

Laura shivered in the cold December air. She hadn't wanted to risk drawing attention to her departure by grabbing her coat, and even though Gee Whiz was only across the street from The Stomping Ground, by the time she reached the door her arms were covered in goosebumps and her teeth were chattering.

She pushed open the door, stepped thankfully into the warmth of the lobby, and began crossing over to the door marked Bar and Restaurant. And stopped. All the time she had been dancing with Jon and working out just how she was going to make sure she saw Simon again, her imagination had jumped from the moment she escaped from The Stomping Ground to the instant that Simon's face lit up with unrestrained joy at seeing her. To the bit in between she had given very little consideration. She certainly hadn't planned on having an obstacle placed in her path before she even got into the room, least of all an obstacle as large and as pompous as Jon's father.

Henry Joseph, his back to Laura, was leaning against the doorpost, deep in conversation with Jemma's dad. Or at least, he was holding forth and Andrew Farrant was opening and closing his mouth at intervals in an attempt to get a word in edge-ways.

"So I told her straight—after all, one can't put these things off for ever, can one, old boy?" he boomed. "You'd be the same in my shoes, wouldn't you, old chap?"

"Er, well, I suppose . . ."

" 'Course you would, no doubt about it. After all, you wouldn't be doing what you're about to do if you hadn't got an eye to the future, would you?"

Laura bit her lip. If she pushed past Mr. Joseph, he'd want to know why she was here and where Jon was and, with a voice like his, the whole room would end up spotting her. She needed a really good excuse for being here—and an even better one for getting into the kitchen.

"That's true," said Andrew Farrant, shifting his position and turning towards the lobby, where

Laura was standing. She stepped hastily behind the hatstand and willed them to shut up and move away.

"One has to change to grow," continued Mr. Farrant.

"Precisely my sentiments," bellowed Henry. "That's where Anona falls down, you see. Set in her ways—typical female, all emotion, no logic."

Pompous git, thought Laura.

"Claire's pretty much the same," said Andrew. "But now we've decided to have another baby, that's all she thinks about."

Laura almost choked. Did Jemma know she was about to become a big sister for the fourth time? It seemed pretty weird that Mrs. Farrant would actually want to go through all the throwing up and getting fat and changing nappies bit yet again. Mr. Joseph, it seemed, was of the same opinion.

"I don't think," he said, "that I could face that at any price. I couldn't go through these teen years again—I don't think these kids know the stress they cause."

We cause stress? thought Laura impatiently. If you two don't shut up and get out of my way, I could well expire with frustration.

"Jon's no trouble, surely?" Laura heard Andrew say. "What does he think of your plans?"

Plans? thought Laura. What plans?

Henry took another swig of wine and began moving back towards the restaurant door. "The boy? Haven't mentioned it yet—having enough trouble with Anona. Anyway, it's not up to him, is it? What about your kids?"

Andrew shrugged. "Like you—haven't told them yet. No point till it's all finalised—and the way Jemma is right now, it's bound to lead to a shouting match. Everything else does."

This is proving interesting, thought Laura.

"It won't do her any harm to have to fit in with other people for once," declared Mr. Farrant. "She's getting a bit big for her boots, these days. She never used to be so lippy. Mind you," he lowered his voice confidentially, and Laura had to strain to catch what he was saying, "I think she gets a lot of it from Chelsea and that Turnbull girl."

"Me!" Laura clamped her hand over her mouth to stop herself exploding in rage. The nerve of that man, she thought. Jemma had been a total mouse when she first came to Lee Hill from Sussex; if it hadn't been for her and Chelsea, she'd probably still not know what a disco was, never mind have revamped her wardrobe and got a life.

"Of course," declared Henry, as the two men began to drift back into the restaurant, "it's so often the case with broken homes. Take Laura—parents at logger-heads, new man on the scene, illegitimate baby . . ."

"And they say that Peter—Laura's real father—is fond of the fruit of the vine, if you take my meaning," added Andrew.

Henry shook his head wisely. "It's not right, you know, Andrew, not right at all."

Laura suddenly felt very sick. She wanted to cry. Or to shout. Or to run away. But she wasn't the running away sort. And the tears were stuck somewhere between her chest and her throat. Shouting seemed like the best option.

She shoved away the coats that were shielding her and strode past Mr. Joseph and Mr. Farrant through the door to the restaurant. Wheeling round to face them, she looked directly into Jon's father's eyes. Henry stopped with a sharp intake of breath, and a flood of colour spread across his already ruddy cheeks.

"What is not right, Mr. Joseph, is the bigoted attitude of people like you!" she hissed.

"Ah, Laura. Well, well. Disco over? Jon with you?"

"Laura, I don't think that . . ." Jemma's dad, flushed with embarrassment, tried to fix an understanding yet reprimanding expression on his face.

"No, Mr. Farrant," replied Laura, with a catch in her voice, "that's quite right. You don't think. You know nothing about my family. How dare you say things about them!"

Mr. Farrant's eyes widened alarmingly. "What the blazes . . ."

Laura swallowed. She thought she might have just possibly gone too far. Out of the corner of her eye, she saw her mother hurrying towards her. Now she was really for it.

"Look, Laura," gushed Henry, who had obviously also spotted Ruth's approach, "you got the wrong end of the stick. I can explain . . ."

"Please don't bother," said Laura. "I understand perfectly."

"Has anyone seen Laura?" asked Jon, as the hands of the clock on the wall edged nearer to midnight. "I can't find her anywhere."

"She was here a while ago," said Jemma.

"I know that," said Jon, who had finally worked out his amazing declaration of love, word for word, and needed to deliver it to Laura right now, before he forgot it. "She told me to dance with Chelsea because she was so out of things and . . ."

"Oh thanks," muttered Chelsea. "Thanks a bunch."

"Well, I mean, I wanted to and all that, but . . ."

"Forget it," said Chelsea and went to the loo.

"That," said Jemma, "was not your most tactful moment."

"That was a horrible thing to say," said Sumitha.

"Nerd," said Bex, and followed Chelsea to the loo.

Oh terrific, thought Jon. Great evening this is turning out to be.

"I'm sure I heard the word 'baby,'" gasped Ruth, grabbing Laura and pulling her to one side, oblivious to the stares and red faces of Henry and Andrew. "It's not Charlie, is it? Laura, what is it? What's happened?"

"Oh, Mum," said Laura, bursting into tears.

"Darling! What ever is it? It is Charlie, isn't it? I

knew I shouldn't have left him, I just knew."

"No, it's not Charlie!" shouted Laura. "Can't you think of anyone or anything other than that baby?"

Ruth frowned. "So what is it?"

Laura couldn't tell her. It would hurt her too much. She thought fast. "I've lost my bracelet," she said sorrowfully. "My lapis lazuli one that Dad gave me. I came back to see if it was here."

Ruth sighed with relief.

Laura noted the way Mr. Joseph's shoulders sagged with equal relief.

"Oh, darling, is that all?" Ruth said. "I thought something terrible had happened. Look, why don't you get back to the disco? I'll tell Barry to get young Simon to keep his eyes open when he clears up."

"Simon?" said Laura, trying to look as if she was searching her memory to place the name.

"The young lad helping Barry—you remember, he carried the haggis in."

Laura beamed at her mother. "Oh him! That's a brilliant idea—I'll go and ask him."

Her mother frowned. "I wouldn't, sweetheart— he'll be busy clearing up in the kitchen. Laura! Come back."

But Laura was already crashing through the door marked "Staff Only."

"I don't know what you're crying for, Chel," said Bex, ripping off some more loo roll and handing it to a snivelling Chelsea. "Do you fancy him?"

Chelsea blew her nose and tossed the tissue into the bin. "Of course I don't fancy him," she said. "It's just that he was right. I do feel out of things. At home, at school, here. Everywhere." She gulped and shook some stray bits of hair out of her face.

"Come off it," argued Bex, peering into the mirror and squishing a zit on her chin. "You? You've got it made. Swish house, stunning looks, adoring parents . . ."

"Oh yes?" said Chelsea. "So adoring that they never even bother to ask what it's like for me, just spend all their time nagging me to do better. And I don't think I can," she added softly.

"But you're mega brainy," protested Bex.

"Don't you start," pleaded Chelsea. "Okay, I used to be fairly bright. But not anymore. I really am dreading these mocks. I know I'm going to fudge them totally."

"Everyone does," interrupted Bex. "The teachers . . ."

"I know, I know, they mark you low to make you worry," chanted Chelsea. "Well, they needn't bother. I'm already worried."

"So what's that got to do with feeling out of things?"

Chelsea sighed. "There doesn't seem any point to anything," she said. "It's like all my friends are moving on and I'm standing still—Laura and Jemma know exactly what they want to do with their lives—Jemma's got offers of acting work even now and Laura's going to be a writer, Jon's all set to be an artist . . ."

"I thought someone said you wanted to be a vet," said Bex.

"That was when I was a kid," corrected Chelsea. "Before I knew it meant six years of studying and doing messy things up cows' bottoms. Now I don't have a clue about what to do at uni. Or even," she added quietly, "if I want to go at all."

"So why think about it?" reasoned Bex. "You can't do anything till June and by then something amazing could have happened."

"Nothing even halfway amazing," said Chelsea morosely, "ever happens in my life."

"Oh puh-leese!" teased Bex. "Chill out a bit, go with the flow. You'll get there in the end."

"It might help," said Chelsea, "if I knew where 'there' was."

Limelight and Letdowns

The kitchen was empty. Laura's heart sank. He'd left already. He'd probably gone to meet his girlfriend, who was quite possibly tall and willowy, with perfect skin and a whole wardrobe full of alluring clothes.

She kicked a pine stool, partly out of disappointment and partly in an attempt to get rid of the knot of anger which was sitting on her chest. Adults could be such total morons, labelling everything and assuming that, just because your dad had left home and your mum had a baby by a new man, you were automatically going to fall apart at the seams and become A Bad Lot.

She bit her lip and blinked hard to stop the tears falling. "Sugar, sugar, sugar!" she muttered, thumping her fist on the table.

"Top cupboard, left-hand side." The voice behind her was musical and distinctly amused.

She spun round. Simon emerged from a huge, walk-in larder, clutching a couple of champagne bottles. Her heart went into overdrive.

"Oh! Hi! What did you say?"

"Sugar—top cupboard," he said, dumping the bottles on the scrubbed pine table.

"Oh. Right. No, I meant . . ." her voice trailed off.

Simon grinned. "I'm teasing," he said easily. "What's the problem? I thought you were rocking over the road."

"I was," said Laura. "I mean, I am. Well, I should be."

This was not the way she had meant it to be. She had imagined herself being suave and cool and piercingly witty.

"You're at Lee Hill, aren't you? Year eleven?" said Simon.

She nodded.

"Thought so," he said. "You used to write really neat stuff in the school magazine."

Laura stared at him. "You read it?"

"Well, of course I read it," he said. "That's what most people do with magazines. You're good."

Laura's heart leaped out of its normal resting-place and landed somewhere near the back of her throat.

"So," pressed Simon, "if it's not sugar you are looking for, what is it?"

Love, thought Laura. And I think I just found it. "I lost my bracelet," she lied. "I just wondered whether you'd seen it."

Simon immediately looked concerned.

"No, I haven't—but I'll look out for it. What's it like?"

"Blue—lapis lazuli, actually. It's got my name engraved on the clasp."

"Lorraine, isn't it?" asked Simon, peeling the foil off one of the champagne bottles.

"Laura."

"Oh yes, that's it, *Rose cheeked Laura, come, sing smoothly with* . . . Can't remember the rest!"

Laura's eyes widened. "What did you say?"

Simon flushed a brilliant shade of scarlet and busied himself with the champagne glasses. "Oh, nothing—it's just some poem we did in English," he said. "Campion or some such."

"You like poetry? Really?"

"Yes," snapped Simon. "What's so odd about that?"

"Nothing," Laura assured him. "I think it's brilliant. Who's your favourite?"

"Well, I love Keats."

"Me too!" exclaimed Laura. "He's so romantic and he sees things ordinary people never notice."

Simon nodded. "And I like Wilfred Owen and the war poets, because they are so sad . . ."

The door behind them suddenly swung open.

"You'll be sad, Simon lad, if you don't get on with pouring that champagne!" Barry Gee said with a grin. "Hello, Laura love—what are you doing here?"

At that moment, a flash of pure inspiration hit Laura in the mid-temple area. "Well, actually, Mr. Gee," she said in the polite voice guaranteed to get parents wishing their own child was so humble, "I had wondered if Simon wanted to come across to The Stomping Ground for midnight—there's a really funky band on. But, of course, I suppose you need him here."

She inclined her head slightly to the right, looked him straight in the eye and smiled a half smile.

"Oh, go on then," said Mr. Gee with a grin. "You're only young once. You two go and have some fun."

"Thanks, Mr. Gee," said Simon, then turned to Laura. "But shouldn't we look for your bracelet?"

She shook her head. "I've just remembered," she said. "I never wore it in the first place. Silly me."

"I've never been here before," said Simon, hanging over the balcony and watching the dancers below. "It's cool."

"It's not bad," agreed Laura, sliding her hand ever so slightly along the balustrade in the hope that he might take it. He didn't.

"Where are all your mates?" asked Simon. "And Jon—you're with him, aren't you?"

"Oh, only sort of," she said hastily. "Nothing heavy."

I'll save the heavy stuff for you, she thought.

"Nice guy," said Simon. "You two look good together."

This is not what I want to hear, thought Laura, tossing her hair in what she hoped was body language for I'm Very Available.

"So, let's go and find the other guys then," suggested Simon, resting an arm lightly on her shoulder.

She shivered in ecstasy. And hesitated. It was

one thing to be up here with Simon, where none of the others would see her, but she didn't want to upset Jon, not on New Year's Eve, not until she could tell him gently and compassionately that she had outgrown him and moved on.

"Why don't we stay up here and watch?" she began.

Simon put his hands on her shoulders. She shivered some more.

"Watch?" grinned Simon. "I would have thought you'd have wanted some of the action."

He playfully flicked her hair and Laura suddenly understood why Jane Austen's heroines used to swoon with delight.

"Oh, I do," she said.

"Well, the action," said Simon, jerking his head towards the band, "is down there. Come on."

"Happy New Year, everyone! Happy New Year!"

The final stroke of midnight rang out from Big Ben on one of the huge TV screens suspended from the ceiling of The Stomping Ground. Party Poppers zapped through the air, balloons popped and everyone hugged everyone else.

Everyone except Jon. He was rooted to the spot,

staring at one of the huge screens suspended from the ceiling. Not the one showing Big Ben. The other one. The one on which Laura was shown in close-up with Simon Stagg. Simon flaming Stagg, who was fiddling with her hair, and getting far closer to her than he should. I'll kill him, thought Jon.

On the screen, Laura's face broke into a radiant smile. A much more radiant smile than any she had directed at Jon throughout the entire evening.

That does it, he thought. I'll sort him.

"Happy New Year, Jon!" cried Chelsea, letting off a streamer over his head.

"You and Laura not seeing in the New Year with one of your marathon snogs, then?" teased Jemma.

"Get lost," said Jon.

"It's Paper Turkey—a new sound for a new year!"

Seb, Tate, and Ross leaped on to the stage and began playing. The atmosphere in the room was electric, with everyone on the dance floor, regardless of whether they had anyone to dance with or not.

Sumitha began clicking her fingers and moving

with the music, her eyes never leaving the guys on the stage. The problem was, they weren't moving enough, weren't filling the stage. They should've been really funking it up, thrusting and swaying, but they were too rigid. The more she watched, the more it annoyed her. Tate had a great voice, but this was dance music, for heaven's sake. So dance, she thought.

Afterwards, she couldn't remember quite how it happened. One minute she was on the dance floor with all the others, and the next she had jumped up on to the stage and begun dancing. Really dancing. The sort of dancing that came when you had spent eight years at The Olive Ockley School of Dance and Drama, doing jazz exams, and stage and tap. The music took over; she caught sight of Tate's astonished expression and then the great grin of delight that spread over his face as the audience caught the beat and began imitating Sumitha's every move.

"Wow!" breathed Chelsea, clicking her fingers and trying to copy Sumitha's foot rolls. "Can she dance!"

Ross and Tate loosened up and began moving around the stage.

"Where *did* she learn that?" said Bex, as Sumitha did a jump split in the air. "That girl's a pro!"

"Stunning!" whispered Simon to Laura, tapping his foot to the beat. "Absolutely stunning!"

Excuse me, thought Laura. It's me you're supposed to find irresistible.

I'll give him stunning, thought Jon, as he pushed his way up to Laura.

"Laura's with me," he said, glaring at Simon. "Come on, Laura, let's dance." He grabbed her hand, hoping he looked masterful.

Laura swallowed. She wanted to spend these last moments with Simon. He hadn't asked for her phone number yet, or said he'd like to see her, or even taken her hand.

"Jon! Hi, good to see you again!" said Simon, with a broad grin. "Didn't know you were the dancing type. See you, Laura."

Terrific, thought Laura. He might have fought a bit harder for me.

"What were you doing with him?" asked Jon.

Laura was about to tell him that it was none of his business who she was with, when she caught the expression on his face. He looked worried and lost and rather small.

"Oh, I lost my bracelet and I went back to see if he'd found it," she said. "And Chelsea's dad said he could come over—I couldn't leave him on his own, could I? He doesn't know many people."

Jon smiled with relief. "You really are a kind and understanding person," he said. And kissed her.

Apart from another stab of guilt, she still didn't feel a thing.

On stage, Sumitha was really into it, step kicking and knee hopping as the audience clapped to the beat. She felt on a real high. She had forgotten just how good dancing made her feel, how it drove everything else from your mind and left you feeling as if you could conquer the world.

Just as the band crashed out the final bars, Sumitha spun round and did the splits, throwing her arms wide open. The audience erupted, stamping feet and giving wolf whistles.

"Brilliant!"

"That was ace!"

The band downed instruments and joined in the applause.

"You were fantastic!" cried Seb. "You're what we need—the fourth man!"

"You really got the crowd going," said Tate. "You'd be wicked."

"Mega," said Ross, which for him was quite an outpouring.

Sumitha glowed. She hadn't felt this good, this full of confidence, in ages. She was beginning to wish she hadn't dropped all her dance classes. And to think she did it on the spur of the moment, just because she'd had a childish crush on Mr. Sharpe and wanted to get straight As in science. But physics didn't give you a buzz like this. Nothing gave you a buzz like this. This was living. It would be so cool if she could join the guys, but that was just a wild dream.

Before she realised what was happening, Tate and Seb had swept their hands under her arms and lifted her high in the air. Everyone laughed.

"So will you?" Seb shouted, beaming up at her. "Will you join us?"

Sumitha, still pulsating with excitement, shook her head, laughed with them, and executed a high cross kick in the air. And another. And another.

"SOOOO-MITHA!"

The laughter died. Heads turned.

"Uh-oh," whispered Chelsea to Jemma. "Not good news."

Standing in the doorway was Sumitha's father. And he was not looking at all happy.

"Hang on, Sumitha! Don't go!"

Seb rushed up to her and grabbed her arm.

"Look, about this idea—" he began. "I thought . . ."

"I suggest, young man, that you keep your ideas to yourself," said Mr. Banerji, proprietorially removing his hand from Sumitha's arm. "Come, Sumitha."

"Dad!"

Seb looked taken aback. "Sorry—I'll call you, Sumitha—okay?"

"It is most certainly not okay," said her father. "If you think that after that—that display just now, I would allow you to have anything to do with my daughter, you are very much mistaken."

Seb looked him straight in the eye, opened his mouth, closed it, shrugged, and walked away.

"I don't believe you just did that, Dad!" hissed Sumitha as Mr. Banerji ushered her through the lobby. "In front of all my friends—how could you?"

She glanced over her shoulder to where the others were whispering and looking anxiously in her direction.

"I hardly think, Sumitha, that you are in a position to question my behaviour," replied her father. "That display on the stage. Had I not arrived at that moment . . ." He shuddered at the horrific memory.

"Your friends—where are they? I told them to come at once," he added impatiently.

"Give them a chance—they're coming!" snapped Sumitha. "Although, after the way you spoke to them, I doubt they'll be my friends any longer."

"Well, get your coat and be quick about it!"

Sumitha felt like crying. It was one thing for her close friends to get the sharp edge of her father's tongue, but at least they knew how totally irrational he could be. But for Seb to have seen her frogmarched off like some dorky kid was more than she could stand.

"It is your association with friends such as these that has brought you to this state," her father said as she walked sullenly by his side on to the street.

"This state? This state?" she spluttered. "All I do is dance—you know, what normal people do at parties—and you go ape and talk as if I've caused grievous bodily harm to a passing old lady. You're so unbelievable!"

She shivered as the cold night air hit her.

Mr. Banerji paused at the kerbside and turned to beckon to the rest of the gang, who were ambling out of the club, trying to look like cool dudes and not wimpy kids who did whatever someone's dad told them to do.

"Keep up, children!" muttered Chelsea mockingly.

"He's even worse than my mother," remarked Jemma, "and that is saying something."

"Is he ever going to shut up?" Jon asked Laura, keeping his arm firmly round her shoulders and making sure that Simon was nowhere near.

"I have made many concessions for you, Sumitha," Mr. Banerji was heard to intone, as the others caught up with a miserable-looking Sumitha. "I permit you to attend these—these places." He paused, as if an unpleasant smell had wafted past his nostrils. "But I will not tolerate a daughter of mine making a public exhibition of herself."

He waited for a stream of traffic to pass. "The time has come for me to take steps."

At that moment, the traffic cleared. From the pavement opposite came the sound of high-pitched laughter.

"Dah-dadadada dah-da, dah-dadadada dah-da, da dah-dah-der, da dah-dah-der . . ."

Jon spluttered into barely suppressed giggles. Laura clamped a hand over her mouth and stole a glance at Mr. Banerji. Jemma opened her mouth and blinked.

Pouring out of the doorway of Gee Whiz were the parents. Doing a conga. With paper hats on their heads. And stupid grins on their faces.

"Hi, cherub!" Mrs. Farrant waved a cracker in the air.

Take her away, someone, prayed Jemma. Like now.

"Happy New Year, kiddos!" called Henry Joseph, whose grasp of the finer points of footwork appeared to be sadly lacking.

Jon closed his eyes and pretended he wasn't there.

Laura groaned, as Melvyn gyrated down the street, a tablecloth tied, turban-style on top of his head and a pair of spoons in one hand, which he was using as maracas.

Sumitha's mother, purple sari gripped in one hand, was bringing up the rear, laughing uncontrollably. When she caught sight of her husband, she stopped.

"Dad," said Sumitha, through gritted teeth.

"Yes?"

"What was that you were saying about public exhibitions?"

For once, Rajiv Banerji was lost for words.

Midnight Musings

7

Sumitha rolled over in bed and slammed her fists into her pillow. Thanks to her father, everything had gone wrong; there was no chance Seb would ask to see her again—her father was hardly the kind of person you messed with if you didn't have to.

Why did he have to be so stuffy? After all, it wasn't as if she didn't try to please him. She worked hard, she endured long family parties during which everyone went on at great length about how great Calcutta was and how terrible Western society was—until she wanted to explode and ask them why they didn't all go home if India was so perfect. She even kept all her teenage magazines hidden at the back of her wardrobe because her father thought them depraved. But she didn't see why she had to miss out on every chance of fun just because her father lived in the Dark Ages.

All the way home in the taxi he had gone on and on about morality and conducting oneself with decorum and not copying Western ways of behaviour. And then, just as she thought he had actually finished and was going to let her go to bed, he had dropped the bombshell.

"From now on, Sumitha, I am banning you from attending these discos," he said. "They encourage you to mix with unsuitable boys and they are not places for a well-brought-up Bengali girl."

She had cried and pleaded with her mother to make him see sense, but although Chitrita had nervously suggested that maybe that was a little hard, her father wouldn't budge.

Well, she thought now, tossing in bed, she wasn't going to let him ruin her life. Anyone would think she had done something really wrong. She did so want to see Seb again. But she didn't have a clue where he lived, or even which college he went to. There was only one thing for it. She would have to find an excuse to call at The Poplars and talk to Tate. She wasn't sure what that excuse would be, or even what she would say when she got there, but of one thing she was completely sure. She wouldn't be telling her parents anything about it.

❀   ❀   ❀

Laura lay on her back, staring at the ceiling and trying to remember every detail of Simon's face. Did he like her? Or was he just being polite? Maybe he already had a girlfriend. A sharp pang of jealousy shot through her ribcage at the thought of anyone else running their fingers through that blond hair or kissing those very full, moist lips.

Suddenly, the thought of term starting in two days' time was hugely appealing. In exactly fifty-four hours' time, she would see him again. She didn't even know what tutor group he was in—but he did English, that much she did know, and if she had to hover outside every year twelve English class for the whole week, she would bump into him accidentally-on-purpose, if it was the last thing she ever did.

She closed her eyes and began dreaming how it would be the day Simon first kissed her.

Jon hadn't even bothered to undress. He had just kicked off his trainers and flung them across his bedroom in fury. He was too angry to sleep. Too angry and too worried.

He could have killed his father. To stand in the carpark of Gee Whiz like that, and say what he said, was just the pits. Just remembering it made Jon shake with embarrassment.

"Time to go, son—aren't you going to kiss the little lady night-night?"

Jon had given Laura a quick peck on the cheek. He couldn't do anymore, not with all the parents hanging around.

"Good grief, lad, you'll have to get a better technique than that if you're going to be success with women!" guffawed his father.

Of course, now he could think of loads of really good replies—like, "I don't have the right role model"—but then he just found himself staring at the gravel and wishing the ground would open and swallow him up. By the time Jon's mother had ushered her husband into the passenger seat and informed him that he was drunk and an idiot, but sadly he would still be an idiot by tomorrow, Laura had gone.

"Not brilliant at picking your girlfriends, are you?" his father had burbled on the way home. "That Suminder girl—not sensible to get mixed up with foreign types—and now Laura. You can do better than her, you know. Far too full of herself. Still, she'll do to practise on."

"That's a terrible thing to say!" Jon had shouted.

"Henry! For heaven's sake!" exploded his mother.

"Well, son, you have to admit that you do need practice!"

"Shut it, Dad," Jon had mumbled.

"Ignore him, dear," his mother had said soothingly from the driving seat. "Forget it."

But he couldn't forget it. What if his dad was right? After all, he was sixteen and a half and his record on the girl front wasn't exactly great. From what his mates at school told him, he had an awful lot to learn about—well, things. He knew that what he felt was real enough—it was just talking about it and doing the romantic bit that girls liked that he was so bad at.

Perhaps that was why Laura had spent so long with Simon—perhaps he had got the right technique. Well, he's not going to get another chance to try it out on Laura, thought Jon. I'll get it right next time, whatever it takes.

Chelsea woke up with a sinking feeling in the pit of her stomach and peered at her bedside clock. Seven thirty. She squeezed her eyes tight shut and tried to fall back to sleep, but the thought of all that home-work lying untouched in her schoolbag made her feel sick. It was only a week until the mock exams. It was all very well for Miss McConnell to say that she would be fine, and that her bad grades last term were just a blip, but she knew her teacher would go all tight-lipped if her holiday homework wasn't done. What's more, her parents would make doomladen predictions about dole queues and wasted opportuni-ties. Term started in two days' time and there was no way she was going to get it all done, not even if her brain finally kick-started itself into action.

She should have got down to it straight after Christmas. It wasn't as though she meant to put it off, just that every time she sat down to start, she got all shaky and hot and knew it wasn't going to work. She had got as far as drawing up a very elab-orate timetable of work, with a different colour for each subject and a little box to tick when the work was done. The ticks were conspicuous by their absence.

Of course, it wasn't altogether her fault. The newspapers were full of features about the bad effects on little kids of having mums who went out to work, but no one stopped for one second to consider the traumas inflicted on teenagers when their maternal parent was never at home. Her mother had many failings, most of them embarrassingly obvious, but she was brilliant at constructing whole essays out of thin air, while laying the table or vacuuming the carpet, and she could dictate an analysis of the war poets or a commentary on the humour of Jane Austen without even breaking out into a sweat. At least today was a bank holiday and her mother could minister to the needs of her highly stressed daughter, instead of spending her time in front of a microphone giving total strangers the benefit of her expertise.

It was no good, she thought, rolling reluctantly out of bed and shoving her feet into her Bart Simpson slippers. She couldn't put it off any longer. Maybe if she sat here in her bathrobe and just wrote the first few paragraphs, it would get her going.

She slipped a sheet of paper from her sociology file and picked up her pen. She read the title. And then read it again. It was stupid—how could she write four sides on that?

She was hungry. That's what was wrong. She'd just go and get some cereal and a banana and then she'd be fine.

She was halfway downstairs when the telephone rang.

"Hello, Leehampton five-five-four-nine-zero-one, Chelsea Gee speaking. No, sorry, she's asleep. Asleep, yes. Who shall I say called? Trudie—oh hi. Yes, I remember. No, she said she wasn't working bank holidays any . . ."

The phone was wrenched out of Chelsea's hand and her mother, clad in a voluminous peacock-blue caftan, across which strode two earnest-looking elephants, shot her a look of thunder.

"Trudie, good morning—Ginny here. She is? You have? Well, of course I'll come in, darling—thrilled to help out. Nonsense—just some silly idea of Chelsea's. You know these young people, living on another planet. See you in half an hour. Ciao!"

She slammed the phone on to the receiver and wheeled round to face Chelsea. "What were you thinking of, talking to Trudie like that? Making me sound so uncommitted."

Chelsea shrugged. "You said on Boxing Day night that you would never, ever work a bank holiday again," reasoned Chelsea.

"Yes, well that was then, and this is now," said

her mother, turning back up the stairs. "Do get out of the way—I must get dressed."

"But Mum, you said you were going to be at home today—I wanted to ask you about my project —it's really hard."

"Later, dear —we'll talk about it later."

"It's always later with you, isn't it? You never have time for me."

Ginny glared. "Oh, don't be so dramatic!" she said. "Of course I do. I'll help tonight."

"Promise?"

"Promise. Now what shall I wear?"

"Preferably," said Chelsea, "something without elephants on it."

"Jemma, Jemma, wake up, Jemma!"

Something hard landed on Jemma's head and something else equally hard bounced on her feet.

Daniel and Luke were wrenching the duvet off her bed and clambering all over her.

"Go away, you horrible lot!" she shouted. "I'm asleep."

"That's a lie, you're awake!" retorted Daniel, who despite being only five, was astute in such matters.

"You shouldn't tell lies," added Luke, his twin brother. "My teacher said."

"The TV's gone all fuzzy wuzzy," said Daniel. "You've got to mend it."

Jemma yawned.

"Go and ask Dad," she said, rolling over and pulling the duvet back over her head.

"We did," commented Luke. "He said if we didn't get out of his sight in two seconds he wouldn't be sponsored for his actions."

"Responsible, silly," corrected Daniel. "So we've come to you."

"And if you don't come, we'll tickle your feet."

Jemma threw back the duvet, stomped downstairs and peered behind the television. The aerial lead was hanging loose. She rammed it in the socket and the picture immediately cleared.

"Wrong channel," said Luke. "We want . . ."

"Wait!" said Jemma, holding up her hand. "I want to see this."

The Zipzap advert showed a puny guy with big specs and a pudding-bowl haircut munching a Zipzap chocolate bar. In a flash, he was transformed into a really fit hunk, Rollerblading up a wall to the admiring applause of a crowd of starstruck girls.

"*I was just an ordinary kid, till I discovered Zipzap bars—now I'm up with the superstars!*" went the background jingle.

The camera zoomed into a full close-up of the newly transformed guy.

That, thought Jemma, could be me. If I had halfway co-operative parents. They have to let me do it. I'd be in all the cinemas and TV screens of the nation. It could be the start of all sorts of amazing things.

"I could be doing that soon," remarked Jemma.

The boys burst into peals of unrestrained mirth, rolling around on the floor and spluttering uncontrollably.

"You?"

Jemma nodded.

"You couldn't Rollerblade for toffee," said Luke.

"Not Rollerblade, dimbo, be in that advert," said Jemma, watching their faces for a flash of admiration.

"Jemma, please go away," said Daniel. "We want to watch the Teletubbies."

Respect and admiration, thought Jemma, are in very short supply in this house.

It was as she reached the top of the stairs that she

heard the low murmur of voices from behind the closed door of her parents' bedroom.

"For the last time, Claire, the answer is no!" she heard her father say. "Jemma has GCSEs in four months' time. They matter a lot more than some tacky television advert!"

"Oh, I don't think it's tacky, dear," murmured Claire. "I rather liked the one with the toddler who was deep-sea diving. Besides, it's Miss Ockley's brother who masterminds them . . ."

"I don't care if Kenneth Branagh is overseeing the wretched thing," asserted Andrew. "Jemma is getting far too wrapped up in all this drama business. Come to think of it, you've changed your tune —only last year you were worried it would spoil her. Well, it has."

Oh, thanks a million, thought Jemma, sinking down on the top stair and straining to hear the conversation. I love you too.

"Anyway, she's going to have far more important things to think about when she knows what's happened."

Jemma frowned. The only thing that had happened in their mega boring household in the last month was that Daniel's stick insects had escaped and were somewhere in the central heating system, probably being turned to charcoal.

"I suppose it is," said her mother. "When are we going to tell the children? They'll be so excited."

That'll make a change, thought Jemma. Not that I should build up my hopes—their idea of excitement is a trip to the garden centre.

"Tomorrow at supper," declared Andrew. "When they get home from school. We'll tell them then."

"And the TV work?" ventured Claire.

"Claire! On this I am unshakeable. Do you understand?"

"Yes, dear," sighed Claire.

My mother, thought Jemma, is a grade one wimp.

8
New Term, New Dilemmas

"**M**orning, darling!" beamed Chelsea's mother as Chelsea dragged herself into the kitchen. "All ready for a new term?"

"No," said Chelsea.

"Now, come along, sweetheart, that's not the attitude," said her mother reprovingly. "Up and at 'em, that's what I say!"

"Along with a whole host of other damned stupid remarks," snarled Chelsea, who was suffering from premenstrual syndrome, exploding zits, and the certain knowledge that today was going to be a very bad day.

"Chelsea! What on earth is the matter with you?"

"Do you really want to know? Okay, I'll tell you. You promised to help me with my sociology essay.

You said that, when you got home from the radio station, you would give me a hand."

"Oh, darling, I know, I am so sorry but, you see, I hung on there because people were dropping like flies with this flu virus, and they needed help with *Live at Five* and . . ."

"Oh well, of course," sneered Chelsea. "Why should I expect that anything I might need should come before your precious radio shows? After all, I am only your daughter—what do I matter?"

"Oh, Chelsea, don't be like that!" pleaded Ginny. "It's very important right now that I make a good impression, am seen to be versatile, willing to muck in, keen to help wherever I can."

"Except when it comes to helping your own daughter," cried Chelsea. "I really needed you, Mum, and you couldn't be bothered. And now I haven't done it, and . . ."

"What do you mean, you haven't done it?" said Ginny. "You've had the entire Christmas holidays to do it. It can't be that hard for someone with your brain. Honestly, Chelsea, you really must learn to manage your time better!"

"What would you know?" cried Chelsea, bursting into tears. "You haven't even bothered to ask what it's about. You just assume I can cope! Well I can't!"

Ginny bit her lip, counted to ten, and fixed a smile on her face. "I'll tell you what," she said as calmly as she could, "how about we look at it tonight? As soon as you get home. We'll crack it, I promise."

Chelsea sniffed. "What will I say to Miss McConnell? You lose five per cent automatically if work is handed in late."

"Stupid idea," muttered Ginny. "I'll write a note—say that it's all my fault and that I picked up your essay in mistake for some work papers, and left it at the office. She won't dare take issue with me."

Chelsea allowed a faint smile to touch her lips.

"Thanks, Mum," she said. "And you positively promise to help me tonight? You won't let me down?"

"Would I?" said Ginny.

"I don't know why Mr. Todd bothers to hold these start-of-term assemblies," muttered Jemma, as they filed into the school hall. "He says the same thing every time—he might as well play a recorded message."

"Or get my father to stand in for him," said

Sumitha. "He's still in overdrive about the disco—says I was debauched and brazen." To her alarm she felt her eyes filling with tears.

"Hey," said Jemma, "you know that's crazy."

"Maybe," said Sumitha, "but I'm still forbidden ever to go to The Stomping Ground again."

"What?" exclaimed Jemma in disbelief. "That's a bit much—even my mum approves of that place, and you know how medieval she is."

"I did enjoy it," sighed Sumitha. "I think Seb is so fit."

Jemma grinned. "Not as fit as Tate," she said.

"You really liked him, didn't you?" asked Sumitha, dropping her voice as Mr. Todd mounted the stage.

Jemma nodded. "And how," she said. "I'd die to see him again, but there's not much chance of that."

That's it, thought Sumitha. That's how I do it. And with Jemma as an ally, it might just possibly work.

Mr. Todd rapped the lectern with a ruler and the room fell silent.

"You'd really like to meet him again?" whispered Sumitha, from behind her hand.

104

Jemma nodded. "Fat chance," she said.

"It can," said Sumitha, "be arranged."

"Praise my soul the King of Heaven . . ."

Where is he? thought Laura. Where's Simon?

"To His feet thy tribute bring."

There! That's him, over there, next but one to Jon.

She shifted her feet slightly, in order to get a clear view between Mandy Fincham's left ear and Warren Timbrell's unfortunate haircut.

"Ransomed, healed, restored, forgiven . . ."

He really was gorgeous. He wasn't like other guys—there was a sort of calm serenity about him that was a real turn-on. It was like he knew who he was and didn't have anything to prove.

"Evermore His praises sing."

She glanced along the row to where Jon was standing and realised that he was watching her. She smiled faintly as their eyes met. And knew. It was no good. She couldn't kid herself any longer. Jon was a very dear friend. But Jon didn't make her toes tingle or send shivers down her spine.

And Simon did.

She was looking at him, thought Jon miserably. I

reckon she fancies him. He's not even that great to look at. Not really. Not unless you go for the pale and delicate weed look.

Perhaps he can snog properly. But they can't have done that. She only met him two days ago.

Perhaps he's good at chatting up. Perhaps he wears sexy aftershave.

Perhaps I'll kill him.

"I'm really sorry, Miss McConnell," said Chelsea, in her meekest voice, at the start of her lesson. "My mother has explained it all in the note."

Miss McConnell nodded, her eyes scanning Ginny Gee's scrawling script. "Very well," she said. "As long as you bring the work in tomorrow I will not deduct marks."

"Thank you," said Chelsea.

"Oh, and do tell your mother how much I enjoyed listening to her phone-in last week—I thought what she said about the importance of parental input in child development was spot-on."

Pity, thought Chelsea, she can't practise what she preaches. "I'll tell her," she said, with a sweet smile.

While her daughter was grovelling to Miss

McConnell, Ginny Gee was preparing to convince Trudie Lambert that her ideas for the new-look Radio Leehampton were unquestionably the best. She had sat up half the night, typing a presentation which she felt sure would prove to Trudie that she was young at heart, vibrant, innovative, and nothing at all like most fifty-year-olds. That she was, in short, indispensable.

She had taken ages to decide what to wear for this restructuring meeting—and could tell by the way the hum of conversation in the editorial office ceased as she walked through, that she must look pretty stunning. Admittedly, the side split on her black, wool sweater dress did seem to go up a little higher than it had in the shop, and the pale-pink feather trim on the neck meant she was constantly fighting the temptation to sneeze, but she thought she combined a look of authority and wisdom with a touch of zany youthfulness. Just, in fact, what Trudie was looking for.

She knocked on the door and walked into the conference room, expecting to find most of the team already in their places. Instead, Trudie sat in solitary splendour at the head of the rosewood conference table.

"Ah, Ginny," she said. "Do come in and have a seat."

"Am I the first?" said Ginny.

"Ah," said Trudie. "Well, I thought we'd have a little chat. You and I. On our own. You see, there are things that need to be said."

The more Sumitha thought about her idea, the more foolproof it seemed to be. Jemma wanted to see Tate; Tate would know where Seb lived. And, if they played their cards right, they could both get what they wanted without admitting they wanted it. It was a cinch.

She didn't share any lessons with Jemma and had to wait until lunch-time before she could talk to her.

"So what do you think?" she asked, as they walked into the canteen, arm in arm. "You come round to my house, and then we go down to Tate's. That way, you see him and I find out about Seb."

Jemma frowned. "I don't know," she began.

"What do you mean, you don't know?" demanded Sumitha, who couldn't be doing with Jemma going all weak-kneed on her now. "You were the one swooning all over him on New Year's Eve."

"It's not that," said Jemma. "Just that Rob said he might phone. He's seemed a bit off since he got back from skiing."

"So he phones—so you're out!" said Sumitha firmly. "It doesn't do to be too available."

"I know," said Jemma, sounding as if she didn't. "Anyway, we can't exactly march up to Tate's door and say, 'Hi, I fancy you and Sumitha fancies Seb—what are you going to do about it?' now, can we?"

"No, silly," said Sumitha, peering into the display cabinet and taking a cheese roll. "It's far more subtle than that. You're doing your survey."

"Excuse me?" said Jemma.

"That geography coursework we all did—you know, 'Does your neighbourhood provide sufficient leisure facilities for all age ranges?' "

Jemma shook her head. "We finished that last term," she said, putting a bowl of soup on her tray. "It's been handed in."

Sumitha sighed. "Yes, I know," she said patiently, "but Tate doesn't, does he? You go up to the door with a clipboard and say it's GCSE research work and can you ask him a few questions. And he says yes . . ."

"What if he says no?"

"He won't say no," asserted Sumitha, dumping her tray on a nearby table. "Let's sit here." She flopped down on a bench and pulled the ring of her can of lemonade.

"What if his mum answers?"

"Stop trying to find problems," ordered Sumitha. "We'll worry about that when it happens. Now, are you on?"

"On for what?" Sumitha looked up to find Laura, pencil jammed between her teeth, balancing a tray and a pile of books.

"Oh," said Sumitha. "Nothing."

Jemma nibbled a fingernail. "Okay," she said as a vision of Tate resting his hand on her clipboard swum before her eyes. "When?"

"Tonight," said Sumitha, who couldn't be doing with waiting any longer in pursuit of true love. "Come for tea."

"Can't," said Jemma. "Apparently I have to be at supper because the parents have something to tell us all."

"Your mum's not pregnant already, is she?" gasped Laura, picking tomato out of her cheese baguette. "That was quick work."

"What?" squeaked Jemma.

Laura gulped. "Oh, nothing—take no notice," she gabbled.

"Laura, tell me," said Jemma sternly.

Laura shrugged. "Just something I heard your dad say at the party—about how they were thinking of having another baby and how well it fitted in with his plans."

"You're joking? And what did he want to do?" said Jemma through gritted teeth.

"Search me," said Laura.

"You must have got it wrong," said Jemma. "Dad's forever moaning about how much four kids cost, without having anymore. Besides, we've run out of bedrooms."

"Well, I'm only telling you what I heard," she said. "You'll find out tonight anyway."

"Terrific," said Jemma.

"So, will you come round afterwards?" persisted Sumitha.

"I'll come," said Jemma. "If Laura's right, I might decide not to bother going home again."

Parental Predicaments

"For heaven's sake, Henry, you're sounding like some second-rate soap opera!"

The strident tones of Mrs. Joseph assailed Jon's eardrums as he unlocked the front door and slung his kit-bag on the bottom stair.

"Oh, am I?" retorted Henry, from behind the closed kitchen door. "Well, of course, I've always been second-rate in your eyes, haven't I? Never quite matching up to your sainted father . . ."

"You leave my father out of this! We're not talking about him, we're talking about you."

"Oh, you grasped that, did you?" retorted Henry. "You've actually understood that we're talking about ME, about MY life, about MY happiness. Well, that is a surprise; I thought we were only allowed to think about what you wanted."

"That's not fair!"

Jon heard his mother's voice wavering on the edge of tears and decided he had had enough. "Can't you two just shut it?" he shouted, pushing open the kitchen door. His father was grasping the corner of the breakfast bar with whitened knuckles and his mother was twisting a tea towel in her fingers and blinking rapidly. "What is going on?"

"Nothing," said Anona.

"Oh, nothing?" said Jon sarcastically. "It sounded like nothing."

"No, Jon, your mother is quite right," said Henry, turning to face him. "It was nothing. After all, what are my feelings, my hopes, my ambitions, in the great scheme of things? Absolutely nothing."

"If you must know," spat his mother, "your father wants to retire." She said the last word as if Henry had just suggested taking the controls of the next moon shuttle.

"So?" said Jon. "What's wrong with that? It's up to him, isn't it?"

Henry threw him a grateful glance.

Anona hurled a plate into the sink. "Oh, so you'd be happy, would you, Jon? Selling this house and moving to a smallholding in some benighted corner of Cornwall? Downshifting, I think your father calls it. Getting back in touch with nature or some equally daft idea."

"What?" Jon gasped. "What on earth for?"

"Is it so unreasonable?" asked Henry. "I just want out of the rat race, want to spend a few years watching the sun rise, smelling the flowers, sailing on the sea."

"Well, you smell the ruddy flowers, then!" shouted Anona. "Only don't expect me to go sniffing them with you!"

"You just don't care, do you?" Henry snatched his sweatshirt from the back of a kitchen chair and opened the back door.

"Hang on, Dad," said Jon. "You can't mean it?"

"Oh, can't I?" snapped Henry.

"Where are you going?" asked Anona.

"Out," said Henry and slammed the door.

Chelsea turned the corner into Thorburn Crescent and noticed, with surprise, that her mother's car was already parked in the driveway. She was never usually home this early. She must have remembered about her promise to help with the essay and made a special effort. Wonders, thought Chelsea, will never cease.

She dumped her schoolbag in the hallway and

went through to the kitchen. Her mother was on the phone and didn't turn round as Chelsea fell over a pine stool and knocked a pile of papers on to the floor.

"Can I speak to Barry Gee, please. It's very urgent."

"Cup of tea, Mum?" enquired Chelsea, who felt that anything which might encourage her mother to write the essay, rather than just throw in the odd idea, was worth trying.

Ginny flapped an impatient hand in Chelsea's direction. "Sssshhh," she hissed.

Charming, thought Chelsea, hurling tea bags into the pot.

"Well, get him to phone me as soon as he's through, will you? Thanks."

She slammed the phone back on the cradle. "Damn!!" she said, slumping down on a stool at the table and running her fingers distractedly through her newly permed hair.

Chelsea eyed her mother. She was looking very flushed and her mascara was smudged all over her cheekbones. "Are you all right?" she ventured.

"Me? Oh terrific," said her mother, hurling dishes into the sink. "Never better."

"Good," said Chelsea. "So, can we start on this essay?"

"Essay?"

"You remember—you promised this morning," said Chelsea.

Ginny sighed. "Oh not now, Chelsea," she said wearily. "I've far too much on my mind to bother with some stupid essay."

"But you *promised*!" shouted Chelsea.

Ginny bit her lip. "Oh, for heaven's sake—what sort of essay is it?"

"Sociology," said Chelsea.

Ginny raised her eyebrows. "These new-fangled subjects," she said moodily. "Soft options, if you ask me."

Considering her mother did something called Ordinary Levels, which sounded mega easy, and didn't even have coursework to hassle over, Chelsea hardly thought she was in a position to comment, but thought it politic not to say anything. At least, not until the essay had been written.

She grabbed her bag from the hall and pulled out a folder. "Just the first paragraph," she said pleadingly.

"Give it to me," said Ginny, putting on her glasses and leaning towards Chelsea. "What's the title?"

"Unemployment and Its Effects on Family Life," Chelsea recited.

Ginny pushed back her chair and stood up. "And I suppose you think that's funny!" she stormed.

"Pardon?" said Chelsea.

"After everything that's happened today," began Ginny, her eyes filling with tears.

"What? What's happened?"

"They—I—oh nothing, just go away and leave me alone for a few minutes. Please."

"But, Mum . . ."

"GO!"

Chelsea went.

Laura had hung around for ages after the end of afternoon school, but there was no sign of Simon anywhere. And to make matters worse, she had missed both buses and would have to walk home. She ambled across the school yard, looking over her shoulder every couple of seconds, in the hope of seeing Simon materialise out of thin air.

"Please, please let him appear!" she muttered. And walked straight into what appeared to be a moving column of plastic boxes.

"Can't you look where you're going?" shouted an irate voice from behind the boxes, which were now flying in all directions across the pavement. "Oh, it's you!"

Laura gasped. As miracles went, this was pretty impressive.

Simon was scrabbling on his hands and knees on the pavement in front of her but, sadly, the look he was giving her could not exactly be described as full of the milk of human kindness.

"Oh gosh, I'm so sorry!" she gasped, ramming her book back in her schoolbag and stooping down to pick up a stray lid. "I was miles away."

Simon's tight-lipped expression gave way to a broad grin and Laura's knees gave way in sympathy.

"It's okay," he said. "It was daft of me to try to walk home with all these."

"What's in them?" asked Laura.

"Sun-dried tomato bread, fish pie, custard tarts," said Simon. "Home economics."

Laura's eyes widened. "You do home ec? You're kidding."

Simon shook his head. "Why not?"

"Well, I thought boys . . ."

"Oh come off it, Laura," chastised Simon. "You're not into stereotypes like the rest of them, are you?"

"Of course not!" said Laura indignantly. "Is that why you were working for Chelsea's dad? Do you want to be a chef?"

"Or a nutritionist," said Simon. "Or maybe a cookery editor on a magazine—I haven't made my mind up yet."

"And I guess I've just ruined all this lot," said Laura ruefully. "I'm sorry—let me carry some of them for you."

Simon looked doubtful. "Which way are you going?"

That, thought Laura, depends very much on which way you're going.

"Berrydale," she told him, praying that he didn't live in the opposite direction.

"Cool," said Simon. "I'm at Byron Walk. How about we cut down the footpath by the allotments?"

Thank you, God, thought Laura silently.

"I hope your mum wasn't expecting to eat this lot for supper," she said, as they turned off the road.

Simon's face clouded. "My mum died," he said softly. "Cancer. Two years ago."

Laura felt awful. "Oh gosh, I'm sorry," she said. "That must have been terrible."

Simon nodded. "It's so hard just watching someone you care about suffering, and not being able to do anything about it," he said. "It makes all the other things you thought were important seem so pointless."

He swallowed hard and looked away.

Tentatively, and not quite certain whether she should, Laura put down her schoolbag and lay a hand on his arm. "You okay?" she said.

" 'Scuse me!" a voice boomed from behind her.

"Watch out!" Simon wheeled round, grabbed her arm, and pulled her against the fence as they almost collided with a large man in a purple sweatshirt and green pants, who was jogging, head down, and making the sort of noise normally reserved for the sound effects of Thomas the Tank Engine.

"Laura!" A red face peered at her in recognition.

"Hi, Mr. Joseph," she said weakly, her heart sinking as she remembered her little outburst at Gee Whiz.

"And the haggis lad!" boomed Jon's father, running on the spot, his face glistening with sweat. "Not deserting Jon, are you, Laura? Not two-timing my boy, I trust!"

Laura cringed with embarrassment and guilt.

"Oh no," intervened Simon. "We're just walking home together."

"Are you now?" boomed Henry. "I'll believe you, thousands wouldn't!" And with that he tugged at his sweatshirt and pounded off round the corner.

"I hope he didn't think . . ." began Simon anxiously.

"He didn't," said Laura. "He never does."

"Now then," said Jemma's mother, after she had dished up large portions of fish pie, "we have something very exciting to tell you all."

Jemma held her breath.

"We're getting a swimming pool!" shouted Samuel.

That'll be it, thought Jemma with relief. Dad's been thinking about it for ages. That would be good for my street cred.

"No," said her father.

"We're going to Disneyland!" cried Luke, through a mouthful of mashed potato.

Better still, thought Jemma.

"Will you just be quiet and listen?" ordered their father.

It is a baby, thought Jemma. Please, not another baby at their age. It's obscene.

"Your father," said Claire, dabbing her mouth fastidiously with the corner of her table napkin, "has got a new job."

Jemma sighed with relief. No babies.

"And so we are going to be moving house," said her mother, rather nervously.

"Neat!" said Daniel.

"Can I have the biggest bedroom?" said Luke.

"No," said Samuel.

"MOVING?" expostulated Jemma. "But we only just got here. Why do we need to move?"

Claire looked at Andrew. He licked his lips and laid down his knife and fork.

"Because," he said, "the job is in Scotland."

"SCOTLAND!" gasped Jemma, pushing away her plate.

"Isn't that exciting?" said her mother, pushing it back again.

"I am not moving to Scotland," said Jemma, "and that is that."

"Oh don't be so silly, petal," said her mother. "It's a beautiful country."

It occurred to Jemma that she didn't sound convinced. "It rains all the time, it's freezing cold, and they eat haggis all the time," she retorted.

"Hardly," laughed her father. "It's a great place—wonderful people, great culture, and the scenery . . ."

"Whatever," said Jemma. "I'm still not going."

Mrs. Farrant stood up and began clearing dishes. "Of course you're going, darling," she asserted. "We're all going."

"But you don't have to worry," said her father hurriedly. "We don't expect you to come up until after your GCSEs."

"Oh terrific," said Jemma. "How good of you. So you all beetle off to Edinburgh, or Glasgow or . . ."

"To Auchinchulish, actually," said her father.

"Okinwho?" said Samuel.

"Auchinchulish," repeated his father. "One of the big Aberdeen teaching hospitals has a research unit there, and I've been appointed to head the ENT department. It's right on the edge of a loch in the middle of nowh . . . in the heart of the country."

Jemma pushed back her chair and jumped up. "Oh great. Not only do you propose to drag me away from all my friends yet again, but you want to dump us miles from anywhere, just so that you can do some stupid research. That is so selfish!"

Her father laid a hand on her arm. Jemma wrenched it away. "And what about my drama? Miss Ockley's putting me in for the audition for *The Darling Buds of May* at the Royal in the summer, and there's the Zipzap advert . . ."

"You are not," said her father, "doing that advert. I've already told you."

"Oh, so it's fine for you to do just what you want, but I mustn't get the chance to even consider doing anything I want, is that it?" yelled Jemma, choking back tears and marching towards the door. "Well, you can forget that!"

Mrs. Farrant passed a weary hand across her forehead. "Your father's taking a lot of trouble to find you a really good school for your A levels, darling," she began.

"Well, he needn't bother," snapped Jemma, "because I'm not coming to Scotland, I am not doing A levels, and I am not going to let you ruin my life!"

She pulled open the back door.

"And where do you think you are going,

young lady?" demanded her father.

"Anywhere that isn't here!" shouted Jemma, and flounced out.

"She's cross," observed Daniel.

"She's really, really cross," agreed Luke.

"She's fifteen," sighed her mother.

10

Postal Predicaments

Sumitha spooned her dessert into her mouth as fast as she dared. All she wanted to do was to get upstairs to her bedroom and reread the amazing letter.

"Sumitha, slow down," admonished her mother. "You will get indigestion. What's the rush?"

"I've got a load of homework to do," she said, smiling in dutiful daughter manner at her father. "Exams in a few days—I can't afford to waste time."

Her father nodded approvingly. "I am glad to see that you are taking your schoolwork so seriously," he said. "Focusing on the important things in life."

"Well, don't work too hard," interjected her mother, clearing away plates. "I am going to fetch

Sandeep from Victoria's house and then I am off to Ruth's for the evening. Girls' night in," she added, by way of explanation.

Wonderful, thought Sumitha. Perfect timing.

"Dad," she said meekly, "Jemma is coming round later—we're working on a geography project together. We have to call at people's houses with a questionnaire."

Immediately her father frowned.

"I told Miss McConnell that you wouldn't want me to do that on my own," continued Sumitha, crossing the second and third fingers of both hands behind her back, "which is why she suggested we did it together."

Rajiv inclined his head. "That was thoughtful, Sumitha," he intoned. "I have no objection to you associating with your friends when it is for sensible ends."

Sumitha smiled and stood up. If he only knew.

Jemma's teeth were chattering. It was one thing to flounce out of the house to make a statement but quite another to do it in the middle of January, just as it was starting to snow. Perhaps she should go home, she thought. Her parents would worry. Then again, she thought, turning the corner from Billing Hill into Sumitha's road, they deserved to worry; it would serve them right.

She felt as if someone had just kicked her in the stomach. She couldn't believe what they were doing to her. It was so selfish. Why couldn't her father just stay where he was, yanking out people's tonsils and shoving grommets in kids' ears, instead of wrecking her life by dragging her off to some god-forsaken hole that no one had ever heard of? Scotland was where they ate that revolting food that Barry had served up on New Year's Eve. Well, she wasn't going, and that was that.

The twins wouldn't want to leave their school; Sam would hate giving up Cubs and judo and Junior League football. And Gran must be devastated—she complained enough about being three hours' train journey away in Sussex, so what she would think about Scotland, Jemma couldn't imagine.

Gran! Of course. She would make them see sense. They probably hadn't even had the guts to tell her yet. In which case, it was up to Jemma to put her straight. Gran was so much more sensible than either of her parents, not that that would be particularly difficult. She would sort them.

"Jemma! My dear!" Jemma had been just about to press the bell when the front door opened and Mrs. Banerji, wearing a black, ankle-length coat and about five scarves, clamped her hands to her head in horror.

"You have no coat! My dear child, you will freeze to death! Come in, come in. And how are you, dear? And your mother? She will be at Ruth's tonight, yes?"

Jemma nodded.

"Such fun we always have. A little—what do you call it? Chin wobble?"

Jemma giggled. "Chinwag," she said.

"Yes, yes, an exchange of news. Not," she added with a sigh, "that much happens here of interest."

"You are," said Jemma, "very lucky."

"Read it, read it!" Sumitha thrust the letter into Jemma's ice-cold hands and hopped up and down in excitement. "Have you read it? Isn't it amazing?"

"Give me a chance," said Jemma, scanning her eyes along the lines.

Dear Sumeefa (is that how you spell it?)

I would have called round but I guess, after the other night, that your dad wouldn't have let me in anyway. He's one uptight guy.

But we need to talk to you about the Battle of the Bands. Tate reckons that you're just what we need—ingredient X he called you! He reckons that if you did a routine like the one you did on Saturday, we'd win, no problem.

Please think about it. Now that we've seen what you can do anyone else is going to be second-best. You are something special.

cheers,
Seb

"Wow!"

Sumitha was pleased to see that Jemma was lost for words.

"Did you read the bit about being something special?" urged Sumitha.

Jemma nodded. "So will you?"

"Will I what?"

"Do it—the Battle of the Bands thing?"

Sumitha sighed and sank down on the bed. "Get real," she said. "With a father like mine? After what he did on Saturday? Considering I'm banned from a regular disco, can you honestly see him letting me dance in a band contest?"

Jemma shook her head. "Not really," she admitted. "Unless, of course, you just don't tell him."

Sumitha chewed her lip. "I just don't think I can go behind his back," she said. "I mean, I know he's a total pain and everything, and there are times when he really gets to me—but Mum says it's only because he cares. In our culture, daughters are protected much more than in yours."

Jemma nodded. "In ours, parents walk all over kids whenever they feel like it," she muttered.

Sumitha stared at her. "Something happened?"

"Only my father aiming to ruin my whole future—oh well, I'll tell you while we walk to Tate's. We are still going, aren't we?" she added anxiously.

"Of course," said Sumitha. "After all, it would be rude not to hear what they have to say, wouldn't it?"

"Very," grinned Jemma. "Very rude indeed."

11
Angst and Agonizing

Ginny Gee revved the engine of her Metro and reversed down the drive at high speed. She didn't really want to go to Ruth's, but anything was better than sitting at home, worrying about her life being over.

How could they do that to her? Axe her radio show at a moment's notice? Ignore all her new ideas? Okay, so her audiences were falling off, but that wasn't her fault; if they had given her a decent time slot, instead of mid-afternoon, when mums were dashing round fetching kids from school and hurtling round supermarkets, she would get more calls.

It was the fault of that wretched Trudie Lambert. Who did she think she was, storming in and changing things? Pompous little cow. Just because she wanted the men at the top to notice her, she thought she could ride roughshod over everyone. Daring to tell Ginny that she wouldn't fit the new, younger, spunkier image of Radio Leehampton.

Ginny brushed away a tear and took a deep breath. This wouldn't do—she didn't want the others to realise how upset she was. Chelsea wanting help with that stupid essay had been the final straw —reminding her that now she was just another unemployment statistic. She hadn't meant to flip, to burst into tears like that—but she couldn't help it. She was Ginny Gee, local broadcaster. People stopped her in the street; checkout girls made comments on her latest show. People respected her.

If she wasn't Ginny Gee, broadcaster, anymore, then who on earth was she?

"Well, if you won't, you won't," said Tate, swinging his long legs over the side of the leather sofa. "But I can't see why not."

"Oh come on, Tate," said Seb, twirling a drumstick. "She's just explained."

Sumitha had been over the moon to find Seb at Tate's house, and rather gratified by the crestfallen expression that crossed his face when she said that dancing with the band was a non-starter.

"Yeah, but surely one night out of the whole term isn't going to muck up exams or faze your father?" Tate persisted.

"You don't know her father," intervened Jemma.

"Strict, your lot, aren't they?" said Tate sneeringly.

"It's just that he cares," began Sumitha and then wondered why she was apologising to this guy. "And, anyway, there'd be rehearsals."

"You didn't rehearse for New Year's Eve," reasoned Tate. "And that was cool!"

"That was just a laugh—but this would be serious stuff," said Sumitha. "I'd need to work out a proper routine . . ."

"I've got it!" exclaimed Seb eagerly. "You take a tape of our song home with you, work it all out, and then we'll only need to get together just before the gig for a practice. You're so ace—we trust you. And that way, your dad needn't know a thing about it."

He grabbed Sumitha's hand. "Say you'll give it a go," he urged. "You've nothing to lose."

Sumitha hesitated. It was so tempting. And Seb would love her for doing it. It was only one night, after all. But her dad would never let her out.

"I could be your alibi," suggested Jemma suddenly. "You could come to my house to practise—your dad would be none the wiser."

"Ace!" said Seb. "The gig's on Saturday week at Leehampton Leisure Centre, so you've plenty of time."

"But that's right in the middle of the mocks!" she exclaimed.

"Sumitha," said Jemma patiently. "They are only mocks. They're not the real thing. And you do have the best brain in year eleven—you're hardly going to mess up because of one night out."

Sumitha took a deep breath. "So where's this tape then?" she said

Seb grinned. "You'll do it!"

"I'll think about it," she corrected him. "I'll let you know."

"We need to know now," insisted Tate.

"No, we don't," said Seb. "We've nothing to lose—we're entering anyway. If we hadn't seen Sumitha dance, we'd be none the wiser."

Tate shrugged and looked sulky.

"He's not as cool as I thought he was," said Jemma, as she and Sumitha walked back to the Banerjis' house. "I think I'll stick with Rob."

Sumitha looked at her in surprise. "I thought the only reason you offered to help me out was so that you could chat up Tate again," she said. "Wasn't it?"

Jemma shook her head. "I know what it's like to have one's dreams thwarted," she said. "My parents are doing their best to wreck my entire life with this stupid Scotland scheme, and I don't see why yours should do the same to you. That's all."

"I owe you one," said Sumitha.

"Oh good," said Jemma. "I was rather hoping you'd see it that way. Now this is what I'd like you to do . . ."

"Thank heavens for some sane company!" Anona Joseph flopped down on Ruth's sofa and gratefully accepted the proffered glass of white wine. "If I had spent one more minute in that house, I swear I would have committed murder!"

"Jon being a teenager again?" queried Chitrita Banerji.

"Jon?" Anona shook her head. "No, he's being relatively civilised—it's Henry. He is driving me mad. He wants to retire."

Ruth frowned. "Well, he is fifty-five, isn't he? Is that so bad?"

"Bad? It's catastrophic," declared Anona. "He wants to downshift. Says he's had enough of the rat race and never-ending stress. Personally, I blame BBC Two."

Four pairs of eyebrows lifted slightly and four heads inclined in anticipation of an explanation.

"All these programmes about the good life and growing your own carrots. Now Henry's got this crazy idea about moving to Cornwall and buying a smallholding and becoming self-sufficient—you know, goats and beehives and recycling tea bags. Can you honestly see me bottling plums?"

The others burst out laughing.

"You're not serious?" gasped Ruth.

"Why Cornwall?" asked Ginny.

"Search me," said Anona.

"Are you going?" queried Claire, nibbling a fingernail.

"No way," declared Anona. "Jon's got A levels next year, I'm halfway through my course and just beginning to get the odd commission and the mortgage is finally paid off. I'm not budging."

"And Henry?" asked Chitrita, who rather envied the way Western women managed to stand up to their partners.

"Oh, he'll get over it—it's just some stupid whim," said Anona airily. "I'm just going to ignore it. Who wants to up sticks at our age, anyway?"

"Andrew," said Claire softly.

Everyone turned in amazement.

"Pardon?"

"Oh yes, Henry said something about it on Saturday," said Anona. "New job, isn't it?"

"Where?" gasped the others in unison.

"Scotland," said Claire. "More money, more prestige, nice house on the edge of . . ." She stopped and burst into tears.

"And you don't want to go?" asked Ruth gently, passing her a box of tissues.

Claire shrugged. "Not much," she said. "And Jemma's even less impressed. She stormed out after we'd told her, says she won't come—when she got back she even said I was failing in my duty as a mother."

"Oh, they all say that!" said Ginny, nibbling a cashew nut. "Mind you, it's a difficult age to move. What about exams?"

"Oh, I'm staying here till the GCSEs are over and then we'll all join Andrew in June," said Claire.

"He's lucky you are so accommodating,"

commented Ruth. "I don't think I'd want the upheaval."

"Neither do I very much," said Claire. "But once we have the new baby . . ."

"You're not pregnant, are you?" gasped Ruth.

"Not yet," acknowledged Claire. "But we're trying."

"Claire!" exploded Ginny, "you're forty-five, for heaven's sake."

"Forty-four," said Claire. "I know, I know. It's risky."

"Risky? It's insane," cried Ginny. "You'd be in your sixties by the time the kid left school."

Claire swung round to face her. "OK OK!" she shouted, which was totally unlike her and caused everyone else in the room to hold their breath. "I know all that—but it's easy for you. You've got a good job, people respect you—and if you moved, all you'd do is get another radio show with another radio station. Me—I don't do anything except raise kids and help out at the crèche. So just what am I expected to do in Auchinchulish?" She stopped and blew her nose.

"I'm sorry," said Ginny remorsefully. "And I haven't." She hadn't meant to let it slip.

"Haven't what?" asked Ruth.

"Got a good job," said Ginny. "Or any job. They fired me. Today. Can I have a tissue, please?"

12
Inspiration Strikes

> ### UNEMPLOYMENT - ITS EFFECTS ON FAMILY LIFE
>
> Unemployment means that there is less money coming into the household and this makes it harder to pay bills.
>
> Unemployment is hard on families because lack of money means that everyone has to

Chelsea wrenched the page from her workbook and scrunched it into a ball. It was no good. She couldn't even write the first paragraph, never mind the four pages that Miss McConnell wanted by tomorrow. There was no alternative but to copy reams of boring statistics from her sociology textbook and put a few extra commas and adjectives in, and hope Miss McConnell didn't notice. But she would. She was like that.

"Ginny! I'm back!"

Chelsea had just written the title for the fifth time when the front door slammed and her father's voice reverberated up the stairs.

"Hi, Dad!" she called, going on to the landing. "Mum's at Ruth's for the evening."

"Oh right," said her father, striding up the stairs two at a time. "What was the problem?"

"Problem?"

"She phoned and I was in a meeting. She said it was very urgent."

"Oh that!" said Chelsea. "I don't know—she was in a foul mood from the moment I got in."

Barry sighed. "The meeting didn't go well then?" he asked.

"What meeting?" said Chelsea.

"Don't you ever take an interest in your mother's work?" asked her father. "There was a big reorganisation meeting on today at the radio station — and I had a nasty feeling that it might not all go Ginny's way."

Chelsea shrugged. "Oh yeah. Even so, she promised to help me with my essay and then, when I showed it to her, she stormed off upstairs in a right miff. So, will you help? Please? To save my life?"

Barry shook his head. "The last time I wrote an

essay, there were dinosaurs at the bottom of the garden," he said. "I'd be no use to you."

"Yes you would," Chelsea assured him. "It's all about unemployment and how it affects people."

"It's about what?" Barry stood stock-still.

"Unemployment and . . . ah!"

Chelsea stared at her father. He stared back.

"And you had told your mother the subject matter of this essay before she got upset?"

Chelsea nodded.

"I think," said Barry, "we now know the outcome of the meeting."

Chelsea shook her head vigorously. "Come off it, Dad," she said. "People like Mum don't lose their jobs. She's really good at what she does. Manic, but good."

"I was good at my job but it didn't stop them making me redundant two years ago, now, did it?" said her father. "Remember what I was like when Frensham's told me they didn't want me anymore?"

"Do I remember?" said Chelsea. "You were permanently grumpy, snappy, irrational . . . that's it!"

"That's what?"

"The essay!" cried Chelsea. "Never mind statistics—I can give them a first-hand account. First you, now Mum—I can write about how my life is being traumatised."

She paused. "Dad?"

"Mm?"

"If Mum really has lost her job, I will still get an allowance, won't I?"

"I guess so," said her father with a wry smile. "If only to get you off our backs on Saturdays while you go out and spend it."

What is rarely appreciated when considering unemployment, wrote Chelsea, *is the traumatic effects on the children of the household, whose own problems are often far-reaching and yet who are expected to endure their parents' mood swings, change in lifestyle, and constant arguing without comment . . .*

This just might work. Chelsea took another swig from her cola can and turned the page.

13
Strong Words

Jon was relieved to find that only his dad was in the kitchen when he went down to grab some breakfast the following morning. Since his parents couldn't be in the same room for five minutes without bawling each other out, it would make a change to eat his cereal in comparative peace.

"Dad, are you really serious about retiring?" he asked tentatively, ripping open the cereal packet.

"Never been more serious about anything," his father assured him. "I'm sick to the back teeth of working in an environment I hate, with people I despise, doing a job that gives me no satisfaction."

"Okay, so retire, but what's all this crazy Cornwall business?"

"New beginnings, fresh start," said Henry, spooning cereal into his mouth at great speed. "What is it your generation is always saying? Get a life? Well, that's what I want—a life."

"A life? Growing vegetables, keeping chickens—sounds like a slow and lingering death to me. Mum will never agree to it, anyway."

Henry looked him straight in the eye. "No, you're probably right," he said quietly. "But that's her choice."

Jon gasped. "You wouldn't just go—without her?"

Henry shrugged and said nothing.

"DAD! Are you out of your mind?"

Henry sighed. "No, I'm not," he said. "But I will be if things go on like this. So, for once in my life, I'm putting me first."

"That is so selfish!" shouted Jon. "Well, you needn't think I'm going anywhere with you, and Mum won't—so you'll be on your own, won't you?"

His father shrugged. "We'll see. Now, are you going to join me for a quick jog before school? The air will clear my head for this confounded meeting."

Jon eyed him. "No," he replied. "And, anyway, you shouldn't go jogging on top of food."

"Oh, I've only had a few mouthfuls," said Henry. "And, besides, I'm only going round the allotments."

He pushed back his chair and carried the bowl to the sink. "Talking of allotments," he said, turning on the tap. "Saw Laura last night when I was out."

"To speak to?" asked Jon anxiously. His father was enough of a liability when his mouth was closed. When it was open he required a government health warning.

Henry nodded. "She was with that Simon guy. Very friendly they seemed to be, too."

Jon felt sick.

"You'd better keep an eye on those two, if you want to hang on to Laura," warned his father. "Mind you, you've never been great with the girls, have you, lad? Not like me!"

Jon bit his tongue and counted to ten.

His father pulled his sweatshirt over his head and opened the back door. "I could always buy you a self-help book, you know," he added with a grin. "Show you how it should be done."

"Oh drop dead," snapped Jon.

Chelsea peered tentatively round the kitchen door. Her mother was sitting at the breakfast table, scribbling on a huge sheet of paper. Of her father, there was no sign.

"It's all right, you can come in," smiled her

mother. "I won't bite your head off."

"Have you—I mean, did they . . .?" began Chelsea, who, after sitting up half the night writing her essay, couldn't be doing with over-emotional mothers.

"They fired me, yes," she said. "They want me to do the rest of this week and that's it." She dropped her eyes and concentrated on her list.

"Don't worry, Mum," said Chelsea, putting an arm round her shoulders. "You've got your newspaper work and . . ."

"That," said Ginny, "is peanuts. Two columns and one feature a week—hardly enough to pay the council tax. And that won't go on forever."

She screwed the top back on her pen and leaned back in her chair. "No," she said decisively, "this is crunch time. I've had enough of being good old Ginny, who'll fit in wherever she's needed; good old Ginny, who always bounces back, no matter what. I've had it with the media. Finished, over, caput!"

Chelsea blinked. "But, Mum, you love the publicity, you know you do."

"Me?" Her mother looked genuinely astounded. "Darling, I shun the limelight, you know I do."

"You," said Chelsea, "would sky-dive into a vat of

tomato soup if you thought a TV camera was on hand to record the event."

Her mother had the good grace to look just a little sheepish. "Anyway," she said, "who is to say I won't end up more famous than ever? I have a few ideas up my sleeve."

"I don't suppose there's any chance of them staying there?" enquired Chelsea.

"Not a hope," said her mother.

"So what does Gran think of this pathetic idea of Dad's?" demanded Jemma, spreading Marmite on a piece of toast.

"Well, actually," said her mother, "we haven't told her yet because . . ."

"I thought as much!" shouted Jemma. "You're keeping a poor old lady in the dark . . ."

"Oh, Jemma, come off it!" smiled her mother. "Whatever your grandmother may be, she is hardly a poor old lady. She tells me she and Tom are thinking of taking up flying."

Jemma scowled. "Well, you may be happy to deceive her, but I shall write to her and . . ."

"You won't have to," said her mother mildly. "She's coming up for a few days while Tom goes on one of his sailing weeks. She arrives tomorrow."

The doorbell rang.

"I'll get it," said Jemma. "I just hope Gran doesn't collapse with shock when you tell her the news. Then you'll be sorry!"

She stormed out into the hall. Claire poured another cup of tea. There were mornings when she felt like something rather stronger.

"Charlie! Don't do that!" Laura leaned across the table and removed a finger of toast from her brother's left nostril. "Honestly, eating a meal with you is enough to put one off food for life!"

"He's experimenting with his five senses," said Ruth. "Psychologists say that . . ."

"Mum?"

"Yes?"

"Shut up."

The doorbell shrilled impatiently and Charlie responded by grinning a gappy grin and stuffing the toast in his right ear.

"I'll get it!" called Melvyn, from the top of the stairs.

"I must admit," said her mother, pouring a second cup of tea, "adorable and amazing as Charlie is,

I don't think I'd want another one."

"Thank heavens for that," murmured Laura.

"Claire must be crazy," added her mother. "Especially at her age."

"Mrs. Farrant? So she is having another baby? Jemma will go ape."

"Well, no, not yet, but apparently once they get settled in Scotland, she . . ."

"Scotland?" exclaimed Laura.

Ruth looked surprised. "Didn't you know? Andrew's got a new job in Oky somewhere or other. I'm surprised Jemma hasn't told you."

"I rather think," said Laura, "that Jemma didn't know."

"Laura, there's someone to see you." Melvyn poked his head round the door. "Come on in—er, Sam, was it?"

"Simon," said Simon.

Laura leaped to her feet, almost knocking over her mug of tea and wishing that she didn't have a mouth full of toast.

"Hi," said Simon easily. "Sorry to burst in—I just thought we could walk to school. I've got something to ask you."

He's going to ask me out, thought Laura. Oh my

god—I haven't cleaned my teeth. I've got scratty tights on. I haven't done my face. And Simon's so much smarter than most guys at school.

Ruth looked enquiringly at Laura. "I thought Jon was calling for you," she said.

"NO HE'S NOT!" hissed Laura, thinking that she was going to have to move fast if she and Simon were to get out of the house before Jon did call.

"He usually does," commented Melvyn. "Nice boy."

"Well, he's not today," snarled Laura. Why couldn't the man shut up and go to work?

She smiled, in what she hoped was an alluring manner, at Simon.

"I'll just get my stuff —be back in a second," she said.

"Don't rush," said Simon. "I can play with your brother. You are a real cutey, aren't you? What's his name?"

Laura left her mother positively melting into Simon's hands.

"You're here—brilliant!" Jemma held open the front door and gestured to Sumitha to go through to the kitchen. "You know what you've got to say?"

"Considering you wrote it down for me, and then phoned me three times last evening, I do think I have managed to suss it, yes," said Sumitha with a wry grin. "But I don't reckon it will work."

"It has to work!" said Jemma dramatically. "My whole future could depend on it." She opened the kitchen door and nudged Sumitha.

"Hi, Mrs. Farrant, how are you?" said Sumitha brightly.

"Sumitha, dear! What a nice surprise! You don't often call for Jemma."

"Well, no, but, you see, I have this enormous favour to ask you."

Mrs. Farrant wiped her hands on a tea towel and looked expectant.

"I'm auditioning for the Zipzap advert—Miss Ockley put me in when you said you wouldn't let Jemma."

She paused just long enough to allow Jemma's mum to begin to feel guilty.

"Well, you see . . ." began Mrs. Farrant.

"But the thing is," said Sumitha quickly, "I've never done anything like that before and Jemma is such a pro."

Another pause for maternal pride to kick in.

"Well, she is rather . . ."

"And what I suggested to my parents . . ."

Always good at this stage to mention someone deemed responsible . . .

" . . . was that if Jemma came with me next week, she could show me the ropes. It's the acting bit that I'm worried about."

Mrs. Farrant shook her head. "I think it would be too painful for you, petal, wouldn't it? Daddy having said no?"

Jemma ignored the references to petals and daddies and put on a brave smile. "If I can't do it, I'd love to help Sumitha have a go," she said. "And it's only a few hours on Saturday."

Mrs. Farrant's forehead puckered into an anxious frown. "But the exams start on Monday, flower, and . . ."

"I don't have one till the Tuesday," said Jemma, who hadn't a clue when she had one, since the exam timetables were still in Miss McConnell's desk.

"I'm going to miss Jemma so much," sighed Sumitha, for good measure, trying to make her bottom lip wobble. "Scotland seems so far away."

Mrs. Farrant smiled sympathetically.

"Oh, well, I can't see why not," she said. "Since it's Sumitha. Now I must dash upstairs and chase up those boys. It's almost eight o'clock."

She bustled off upstairs and Sumitha winked at Jemma. "Yes!" they whispered in unison, slapping hands. "We did it!"

Laura and Simon were almost at the school gates and he still hadn't asked her. They had talked a lot; she had discovered that he was doing English and biology as well as home ec, that he lived with his dad and his grandmother and that he had an older sister who didn't seem to like him very much. He'd told her that he thought she was really pretty. But he hadn't asked her out.

"So, what was it you wanted to ask me?" she said in desperation, as they crossed the main road.

Simon flushed. "Well—I mean—you and Jon, are you really an item?"

Laura shook her head vigorously. "We were," she admitted. "But I'm going to be telling him; it just isn't working."

"So, if you were to go out with someone else, it wouldn't wreck anything?"

Laura's heart thudded. "No," she said. "Except

that I'm not going out with anyone else."

Simon took a deep breath. "I wondered if you'd mind—well, would you come round to my house? Tonight? You could stay for supper. Then my dad and gran could see—meet you."

Laura blinked. This was serious stuff. Most guys put off taking you home for as long as they possibly could and here was Simon suggesting she met his folks before they hardly knew one another. He must seriously like her.

"We could go for a walk, or listen to music or whatever you like," he said in what sounded like desperation. "Please say you'll come."

Just try stopping me, thought Laura. "Well," she said, pausing to pretend to give the matter weighty consideration. "Okay—that would be cool."

"Oh brilliant!" sighed Simon, as though the weight of the world's problems had been lifted from his shoulders. "Thanks."

For just one moment, Laura thought he was going to kiss her.

But he didn't.

14
Bad News

By lunch-time, Jon had a thundering headache and felt like smashing his fists into the wall. They'd been together again. He'd seen Laura with Simon at the school gates, fluttering her eyelashes and smiling that crooked little grin at him. And he hadn't been able to do a thing about it because Mr. Cobbett had been yacking on about history of art essays and telling Jon that he should try to make his written work as good as his practical art. By the time he had finished, the bell had rung and Jon had been left to wonder, all morning, just what Simon was suggesting that made Laura look so smug.

"You look happy—not," said his mate Rob, as they headed for the sixth form dayroom to heat up some Pot Noodles for lunch. "What's up?"

"Don't ask," muttered Jon.

"Okay," said Rob cheerfully.

"I reckon Laura's got someone else," said Jon in a

rush. "Three times now I've seen her with Simon Stagg and . . ."

"Simon!" exclaimed Rob. "I can't see that he's much of a threat."

Jon shrugged. "She seems to be hanging on his every word," he sighed.

"I wouldn't worry—someone told me that . . ."

"Jon Joseph! Jon Joseph!" He turned to see Miss Haddock, the head's secretary, wobbling her way along the corridor towards him.

"There you are!" she said, pausing to catch her breath. "You're needed in the headmaster's office straight away."

Jon frowned. "What for?"

"It is not for me to disclose the head's business," said Miss Haddock primly. "But your mother is there."

Jon sighed. She would have locked her door keys in the car yet again and want his. Honestly, he sometimes wondered if she was fit to be let out.

"I think," said Miss Haddock gently, "you should hurry."

"Come in!" Jon pushed open the study door and walked in. His mother was sitting in the big leather armchair beside the head's desk. Her face was ashen, and she was twisting a handkerchief in her fingers.

"Ah, Jon," said Mr. Todd. "Sit down, dear boy."

Jon knew that this was nothing to do with a lost door key. "What is it, Mum?" he asked.

"Now, Jon, it's okay," said his mother in a voice which said that it was far from okay. "It's your father."

"Dad?"

"I had a phone call on my mobile," she said. "He's been rushed to hospital. He's had a heart attack."

"No!"

His mother nodded and blinked back tears. "You must come with me now to the hospital," she said. "As quickly as possible."

The words caught in her throat.

"Jon," she said faintly, "they say he might die."

"Do they want to kill us or something?" demanded Jemma, at the end of the afternoon, hurling her revision notebook into her kit-bag.

"This exam timetable is unreal," said Sumitha. "How can they put art and geography on the same day? Those are my worst subjects."

"Sumitha," said Laura patiently, "you don't have worst subjects. I reckon tonight will be my last night out until the exams are over."

The very moment she had said it she knew she shouldn't have.

"So, where are you going?" enquired Chelsea, slinging her schoolbag over her shoulder.

"Nowhere much."

"Laura!" three voices chorused in unison.

"Simon's asked me round to his house for supper," she said, as nonchalantly as she could.

"Simon? Simon Stagg?" asked Chelsea incredulously, as they filed out into the corridor.

Laura nodded.

"What about Jon?" asked Sumitha.

Laura shrugged. "He's not my keeper," she said defensively. "We're not tied at the hip, you know."

"Have you told Jon?" asked Jemma.

"No," said Laura shortly.

"Don't you think you should?" asked Chelsea. "I mean, if he hears from someone else . . ."

"Well, who's going to tell him?" snapped Laura. "Unless, of course, you intend to rat on me."

Chelsea held up her hands in mock surrender. "Keep your hair on," she said. "I won't say anything.

But I don't think you're being fair."

"Oh get knotted," said Laura.

"Hey, Laura, have you seen Jon?" Rob belted up to her as she passed the door to the art block on her way out.

Laura shook her head. She wished people would stop talking about Jon. It made her feel guilty.

"Haven't a clue, sorry," she said.

Rob sighed. "He got called to the head at lunchtime and I haven't seen him since," he said. "I have a feeling something might be wrong. He didn't come back into lessons."

Laura looked puzzled. Jon wasn't the sort to bunk off.

"I tried ringing his house but there was no reply," said Rob. "Will you be seeing him tonight?"

"No," said Laura shortly. "Homework," she added, to cover her tracks.

"Oh well, I'll phone again later—there's probably a simple explanation. If you catch him first, get him to call me. Okay?"

"Okay," said Laura and began wondering whether the suede mini-skirt or the rather clingy, velvet hipsters would be best for supper with Simon.

15
A Bad Day All Round

Jon felt as if he was in the middle of a very bad dream and couldn't wake up. They had only let him see his father for a few minutes before he was taken to the operating theatre. He hadn't looked like Dad at all. His face had been grey and his lips colourless. As Jon watched him being wheeled out of the emergency room, his mum hanging on to his limp hand, he had wished that he was five years old and could shout, and stamp his foot and cry and say that he hadn't meant it and he didn't want his dad to drop dead, and if he would just get better, he'd never argue with him again.

But he wasn't five, he was sixteen. So he just stood there, digging his fingernails into the palms of his hands, waiting for his mum to come back.

"They say he collapsed at the allotments while he was jogging this morning," Anona had told him miserably, in the taxi on the way to the hospital.

It's my fault, Jon had thought. I should have stopped him running on top of his breakfast. Why didn't I say more?

"It's all my fault," his mother had said with a catch in her voice. "He said he was miserable, he told me he was under stress and I just ignored it. If he . . . if he dies, I'll never forgive myself."

Die? But of course he wouldn't die, Jon thought now. He couldn't. Could he? Hospitals dealt with heart attacks and bypass operations and all sorts of things every day of the week. They'd know what to do. Wouldn't they?

Jon wished he had someone to share this with. This awful, hollow, gnawing feeling. Someone who wouldn't care if he burst into tears or shouted or said he was scared. He felt horribly alone.

He wanted Laura. A lot. As soon as he got home, he'd phone her. She'd come—he knew she would.

Sumitha slipped the cassette into her mini-stereo and pressed play. She took advantage of her parents' absence—they were at Sandeep's parents' evening—to turn the volume up high.

"Push to the Limits" certainly had a great beat and the lyrics were wicked. There was a great rap interlude, which might be tricky to choreograph, but the guitar solo in the middle was made for dancing.

What was she thinking about? There was no way she could do it—not right in the middle of exams. She wanted to do really well and make her parents proud of her and, besides, it would upset her father so much if he did find out. She was still mad at him over the disco ban, but her mum had said that she should try to understand why he said the things he did. She knew that all her Bengali girlfriends and cousins got treated pretty much the same way—but most of Sumitha's closest mates were Western, and it was pretty hard, sometimes, seeing how much freedom they had. On the other hand, when she watched the rows and marriage splits and traumas that went on in some of their families, she thought maybe things weren't so bad for her. In the end, she couldn't just reject her whole culture.

The track finished and she pressed eject. Casting one final, reluctant look at the tape, she put it in an envelope, scribbled an explanatory note to Seb and sealed it. The envelope popped open. She licked it again. Still it wouldn't stick.

"Sticky tape," she said to herself. She ran downstairs and into her father's study. She scanned the desk top but couldn't see it. She pulled open the top drawer.

Lying on the top of a pile of papers was a half-written letter.

My dear Sajjed,

It was so very good to talk with you on the telephone last week and to hear that Asim is doing so well at University. I was even more delighted when you said that you were considering favourably my early approaches with regard to an alliance between Asim and Sumitha and think your suggestion of a meeting is an admirable one. The two young people need to know one another before anything is finalised, and my wife and I will...

Sumitha stood stock-still. She noticed, with almost detached calm, that her fingers were shaking. Her mouth was dry and she could feel her heart thumping in her ears. How dare he! How DARE he! To discuss, to even consider, her future marriage behind her back! To expect her to agree to such an outmoded, stupid, ridiculous idea!

Tears welled up in her eyes. She wouldn't let it happen.

How could they? She tried so hard to be what they wanted—but this was going too far. She slammed the desk drawer shut and ran back upstairs.

What was the point of trying to be fair to her father, when he obviously had no desire whatever to be fair to her? What was the point of trying to be honest, when all the time he was going behind her back? Why should she consider his feelings, when he never thought about hers?

She grabbed a sheet of paper.

Dear Seb,
The track is great. I'm up for it—I'll work out a routine this week and come and rehearse at Tate's. Thanks for asking me.
See you,
Sumitha

She hoped he wouldn't realise that the smudge on her signature was a teardrop.

Laura was beginning to feel rather uncomfortable. She wished the meal would end so that she could be on her own with Simon. From the moment she had arrived at Simon's house, she had felt that she was under inspection. His dad kept saying how great it was to meet Simon's bird, which was an expression that made her want to slap him round the face, and his grandmother said she couldn't believe young Simon had actually got his act together and invited a girl home. And all the time, Simon stared at his plate and hardly said a word.

"So, are you in Simon's cookery class then?" asked his nineteen-year-old sister, Maddie. She said cookery in a sneering sort of way and Simon glared at her.

Laura shook her head. "No, I'm a year below him," she said. "I'm doing GCSEs this year."

"Laura's a brilliant writer," Simon offered, and Laura threw him a grateful glance.

"Not another poetry freak!" exclaimed Maddie. "Do you know, Simon actually reads poems aloud to himself in bed. Sad or what?"

Laura bristled. "I love poetry," she said. "And how can you really appreciate it if you don't read it out loud?"

Maddie raised her eyebrows heavenwards and pushed back her chair. "Made for each other, aren't you?" she said sarcastically. "Two weirdos together."

"Madeleine!" Her grandmother exploded. "Apologise at once!"

Maddie shrugged. "It was only a joke," she snarled, flouncing out of the room.

Simon's father cut a wedge of cheese and beamed at Laura. "So—you're the girl who finally got our Simon going then?" he said.

"Dad!" Simon hissed.

"Slow starter, my boy is," said the obnoxious Mr. Stagg. "Still, he's made a good choice, I'll say that for him."

Simon pushed his plate away and stood up. "Come on, Laura," he said. "Let's go for a walk."

"Way-hey!" said Mr. Stagg.

"Thank you for the supper," said Laura to Simon's gran, pointedly ignoring his father.

"Come again," she offered.

Probably not, thought Laura.

They had said there was no point in staying. The operation would take several hours and they promised to phone the moment there was any news.

When they got home, Jon had made his mother a pot of tea and tried to sound positive and cheerful, and patted her arm when she cried and wished he could do the same.

"I think I'll go next door and see Claire Farrant," his mum had said, between sobs. "Andrew's medical—he'll know just how good this surgeon who is looking after your father really is."

Jon nodded miserably.

"Will you be all right?" his mother asked.

"Of course I will," he said bravely. "I'll probably call a couple of mates."

After she had gone, he went to the phone and dialled Laura's number. It rang for ages before a man's voice answered.

"Hello?"

"May I speak to Laura please? It's Jon."

"Jon! Good to hear from you—but sorry, she's not in right now."

Jon's heart sank. "It's really important," he said and then cursed himself for sounding wet. "That is,

I've got a message for her."

"Well, she's at Simon Stagg's house—I think Ruth has the number. Just hang on a se . . ."

"NO!" Jon felt as if the lump in his throat was going to choke him. "No, it doesn't matter—I'll catch up with her tomorrow. Bye!"

He slammed down the phone.

He stared out of the window.

Simon and Laura. Laura with Simon. At his house.

He needed her. Now. With him.

The bushes in the garden went all blurry. And, since no one was around, Jon didn't bother to try to stop crying.

"Are you cold?" Simon asked anxiously as Laura shivered.

"A bit," she said.

Actually, her fleece-lined jacket was keeping her fairly snug, but she thought a quick shudder was the speediest way of getting Simon's arm round her shoulder. It didn't work.

"I suppose I was a bit dumb to suggest a walk in the middle of winter," he admitted. "But I wanted to get away from my family."

Laura nodded.

"My dad's such a dork," he said fiercely. "I wish he'd just accept me for what I am."

"What, liking poetry and cooking and stuff?"

Simon swallowed and turned to face her.

She smiled and ran her tongue along her bottom lip.

Simon sighed. "Yeah," he said. "All that stuff."

"Chelsea, darling, what do you think?" Ginny Gee swanned into Chelsea's bedroom and did a little twirl.

She was wearing what appeared to be a lurid tablecloth with sleeves.

"Mum, what have you got on?"

"It's a *cheongsam*, darling—very oriental. I'm going for an interview."

"In that?" gasped Chelsea. "What are you proposing to do? Serve in a Chinese restaurant?"

Her mother tutted. "No, stupid," she said. "I'm thinking of becoming a model."

Chelsea spluttered.

"A mature model," added her mother. "For Largesse—they deal in clothes for the larger lady with style."

Chelsea closed her eyes. "Mum," she said, as calmly as she could, "is it within the realms of possibility that you could find a job that didn't involve making a public exhibition of yourself?"

"Like what, for instance?"

"Something that keeps you lying down in a darkened room?" said Chelsea.

"Oh, be sensible," said Ginny.

"Jon phoned," said Melvyn, when Laura got home.

Sugar, thought Laura. "What did you tell him?" she asked.

"That you were at Simon's," said Melvyn.

Double sugar, thought Laura.

"He sounded a bit odd," said Melvyn. "Maybe you should call him."

Maybe I should, she thought. But then he would want explanations and it would get all heavy.

"It's late," said Laura.

"That," said Melvyn, "has never stopped you in the past."

Laura sighed. "I need to revise," she said piously. "I'll see him tomorrow—it can't be that important."

"Chelsea? It's me—Bex."

"Hi—how are you? You've just saved me from the causes of the Vietnam war."

She expected Bex to laugh, but she didn't.

"Listen, can you do me a favour? It's Ricky."

"Has something happened?"

There was a pause. "I don't know. He's phoned me twice in the last three days and each time I know he's wanted to talk about something. Only he never gets round to it."

"And you think he might be in trouble?" Chelsea didn't think there was any point in beating about the bush.

"No—yes—oh, I don't know," snapped Bex. "Sorry. It's just that I'm worried about him. My mum's useless and he's a pretty easily led kid. I don't want him going the same way I did. Please, Chelsea."

"Okay," said Chelsea. "I'll see what I can find."

"Thanks," said Bex. "You're a mate."

16
Rumours and Revelations

"**I**sn't it awful about Jon's dad?" Jemma grabbed Laura's arm as they went into registration on Friday morning.

"Everything about Jon's dad is awful," sighed Laura. "I can't stand him."

"Charming!" said Jemma, "I would have thought that, under the circumstances, you might possibly be a bit more caring."

"What are you on about?" asked Laura.

"Jon's dad had a heart attack yesterday. He had a major op. He's in intensive care."

Laura's mouth dropped open and her stomach turned over. "I didn't know," she said. And remembered what Melvyn had said about the phone call. "Where's Jon?"

Jemma shrugged. "I don't know," she said. "I

think he went back to the hospital with his mum. I thought he would have phoned you."

He did, thought Laura. And I wasn't there.

"I'm doing it," Sumitha said to Jemma over lunch.

"Doing what?" said Jemma, frowning over some ridiculously complicated graph of the population in South America.

"The Battle of the Bands," said Sumitha.

Jemma dropped her book in surprise. "So what's with the change of heart?"

"It's too complicated," said Sumitha, who had spent most of the morning fighting back tears. "So can I come to your house to practise?"

"Yes, of course. Come on Saturday after my audition. It will be some light relief in the week from hell."

"He's a very sick man, Mrs. Joseph," the consultant was saying, leaning forward in his chair and looking at Jon's mother sympathetically over the top of his rimless spectacles. "The next few days will be crucial."

Anona nodded slowly.

"And I have to say," the doctor added softly,

"that if all goes well and he pulls through, he is going to have to make some big changes in his life."

"Like what?" asked Jon.

"Well," said the consultant, "slowing down, mainly. Reducing stress levels, eating sensibly, taking more leisure—but we can talk about all that in a few days' time."

"I wish," whispered Anona, "we'd talked about it before."

Jon swallowed. "The heart attack," he said to the doctor. "It's my fault he had it."

His voice cracked and the consultant smiled sympathetically.

"I don't see how that can be," he began.

"You have to listen!" said Jon, so urgently that his mother looked up in surprise. "I knew he was going jogging on top of his breakfast. I should have stopped him. And I shouted at him—and I told him he was crazy to want to up and off to Cornwall and . . ."

The consultant laid a hand on Jon's arm. "Hang on, hang on," he said. "None of those things caused your dad's illness. The operation showed that he had clogged arteries, a faulty valve—he was a disaster waiting to happen. It's just lucky we got him in time."

"So you think he'll live?"

The consultant sighed. "It's too early to be sure," he said. "But I rather think he will."

Jon couldn't understand why that made him cry more than he ever had before.

There is more to this sociology, thought Chelsea, chewing on the end of her rollerball, than I thought. It really is pretty interesting. She gazed out of the humanities-block window and across the playground, where years seven and eight were having break. To think that every one of those kids is being formed by the environment around him or her. To think that I am the product of, not only my genes, but my parents' behaviour, she mused. Which, come to think of it, is a pretty worrying concept.

She was about to address herself to her essay when there was a scuffle in the playground below. The words "Runt!" and "Weed!" floated up to the window.

She peered to see what was going on. And gasped. The kid being pushed and shoved around was Ricky. And he wasn't even fighting back. He was just standing, shoulders hunched, while the bullies knocked him around.

Bex was right. Something was wrong. And Chelsea knew she couldn't ignore it.

"Is Jon in school?" Laura gasped, rushing up to Rob and Jemma during afternoon break.

Rob shook his head. "He's at the hospital," he said. "I guess he'll come back after the weekend. How's he taking it?"

Laura looked downcast. "I don't know," she admitted. "I haven't spoken to him. I'll call him tonight."

"So you're not with Simon tonight, then?" said Jemma sarcastically. "You sure you can fit Jon in?"

"Oh shut up!" shouted Laura and pushed past them into the science block.

"There's not really anything going on between Simon and Laura, is there?" Rob asked Jemma. "Because, as her friend, I think you should warn her off."

Jemma looked surprised. "Why? What's wrong with him? Has he already got a girlfriend?"

Rob laughed. "Oh no," he said. "That's the one thing Simon Stagg doesn't have."

"So what's the problem?"

"From what I have heard, Simon isn't interested in girls at all," said Rob. "The rumour is that he's gay."

"So what do I do? I mean, do I say something or what?"

Jemma looked pleadingly at Chelsea as they walked home together.

Chelsea frowned. "Surely if he is gay, he wouldn't have asked her out in the first place?"

"That's what I thought," agreed Jemma. "So shall I just say nothing?"

"On the other hand," said Chelsea, "if you tell her, it might push her back to Jon. And I reckon he needs her now."

"Me too," said Jemma. "I suppose I could put out a few feelers—you know, ask her what he's like to snog and stuff."

"Good idea," said Chelsea. "But be subtle."

"As if I would be anything else," said Jemma.

"So that's it really, Mother." Claire Farrant sighed and stared at her mother, who was sitting quite calmly at the kitchen table, slicing runner beans.

"Is it, dear?" said Jemma's gran serenely. "Well,

it's a big change—how have the children taken it?"

"Oh well, the boys are fine, but Jemma—well, she's being a typical teenager."

"How do you mean, dear?"

"Well, refusing to go, saying we're ruining her life, that we're not thinking of her future . . . all that nonsense."

Her mother laid down the vegetable knife and looked up. "Oh, I don't see that as nonsense, dear," she said quite calmly. "I think Jemma has a point."

Claire Farrant's mouth dropped open in amazement. "But it's a lovely house, much bigger than this one, and the neighbourhood is very select and . . ."

"Oh, Claire, for pity's sake!" snapped her mother. "Do you honestly think that, at fifteen years of age, Jemma gives a toss for all that sort of thing? She wants to be with her friends, pursuing her own interests—not stuck in some damp corner of the country with a load of kid brothers and the night-life from hell! What is Andrew thinking of?"

Claire pulled back her shoulders. "He's thinking of our future," she said. "It's a big promotion, much more money, and we've got the boys' education to think of."

Her mother nodded. "Indeed you have," she said. "But you have to think of Jemma too. What of her drama?"

Claire sighed. "Andrew wants her to do A levels—he's rather fed up with all this stage stuff," she admitted.

Jemma's gran raised an eyebrow. "How very dictatorial of him," she said. "I always thought he had more sense. Well," she added, standing up and pulling her cardigan firmly round her ample bottom, "we shall have to do something about him."

"There's nothing to be done," said Claire.

"Oh isn't there?" retorted her mother. "I rather think there's an awful lot to be done. And I intend to do it."

"Bex? It's Chelsea. Look, about Ricky. I think he's being bullied . . . Yes, today. In the playground."

She paused, wondering how much to tell her friend without panicking her.

"I couldn't do anything then, I was in sociology, but I'll keep an eye out for him . . . Of course I promise. And no, there's no reason for you to feel guilty — you've got to work. Yes, call me whenever you want. Take care. Bye!"

☙ ☙ ☙

"Sumitha! How can you possibly work with that awful music blaring out?"

Chitrita Banerji had just returned home from a rather vocal argument with her bank and was not in the mood for rock music.

"Quite well," retorted Sumitha, thanking her lucky stars that she had opened her geography book before starting to work out the dance routine.

"Well, turn it down—your father is due home any minute and you know how he hates this sort of thing."

"Oh, and of course, we all have to toe the line and do what Dad wants, don't we?" shouted Sumitha. "He thinks he can rule my life, your life, everyone's. Well, he can't!"

"Sumitha! What on earth are you on about?"

"He wants to marry me off, doesn't he? He believes in arranged marriages and he's trying to palm me off on someone I don't even know."

"Of course not, he's just . . ."

"Don't lie to me!" shouted Sumitha. "I saw the letter. In his desk."

Chitrita's eyes widened. "You went to your father's desk?" she gasped, with as much horror as if

Sumitha had been caught removing designer dresses from Harvey Nicks.

"I needed sticky tape," she replied. "And there it was. A letter to someone I don't even know, about me and their son . . . oh it's horrible!"

"Sumitha, you've got it all wrong. It was just a preliminary enquiry."

"So you DID know about it!" stormed Sumitha. "And you let it happen! Well let me tell you this. I will never, ever marry anyone unless I want to. So he might as well tear up the stupid letter and save the stamp!"

The front door slammed.

"There's your father now," said Chitrita anxiously. "Please, Sumitha, don't say anything. I will talk to him. I promise."

Sumitha glared. "Well, don't think he can get round me, because he can't!" she said. "I've had it with the old ways once and for all."

The phone rang and rang. There was no reply. Laura hung up and nibbled a fingernail. She knew Jon's mum had a mobile phone but she didn't have a clue what the number was. And anyway, she could hardly phone if they were at the hospital. She wouldn't know what to say. Suppose Mr. Joseph had died? She'd never known anyone die before—not anyone she knew really well. What did you say? How would it be?

He wouldn't die. Of course he wouldn't die.

She'd ring tomorrow. After all, there wasn't anything she could do. And, besides, she had to get on with her homework because Simon had asked her out the following evening. She knew she should speak to Jon—but then, he wouldn't be going anywhere, not while his dad was so sick, and what he didn't know couldn't hurt him. She'd wait. That would be best.

She had only just hung up when the phone rang again.

"Hi, Laura, it's me—Jemma. I was just wondering how you and Simon were getting on."

Laura frowned. She couldn't imagine why Jemma should suddenly be so interested.

"OK," she said non-committally.

"So have you—you know, kissed and stuff?"

"Jemma!" protested Laura.

"Sorry—but I mean, have you?"

"No, as it happens," admitted Laura. "I'm trying to play hard to get." She wasn't about to let on that

Simon hadn't so much as brushed a lip against her cheek yet.

"So he's really coming on strong, is he?" asked Jemma.

"Oh yes," said Laura. "But I have to be sure, don't I?"

"Mmmm," said Jemma. "Okay, then. Bye."

Laura was left wondering just what that had all been about.

17 Confrontations

"**N**ow, you've all seen the Zipzap adverts, I have no doubt," said Miss Ockley, beaming at the assortment of pupils she had mustered for the audition. "This is my brother, Oscar, whose brain-child they all were."

She glanced affectionately at a rotund man with a ginger beard and hair that appeared to be suffering from the effects of an electric shock.

"He looks like something out of *Dr. Who*," muttered Jemma to Sumitha.

"Hi, there!" he said. "You know that all the Zipzap ads show a magical transformation from being an ordinary kid before you eat a Zipzap bar to becoming a superstar afterwards."

They all nodded.

"Well, this time we're adding a twist. This ad is for new ZipzapLite—the magical, low-calorie chocolate bar!"

He held up a fistful of chocolate bars in lurid pink wrappers. "We're having a mega ordinary kid—sticky-out teeth, nibbled nails, spots, lank hair, plump figure—chewing on the bar and flicking through a teen magazine."

Jemma frowned. That didn't sound very glamorous at all.

"Then, pow! she is transformed into this gorgeous, slender creature, with flawless skin, bouncing hair and radiant smile, stalking down a catwalk, wearing the latest see-through number, while the flash bulbs explode around her!"

A murmur rippled through the half-dozen girls waiting to audition.

Jemma frowned.

"Right, who's first? You?" he pointed to Sumitha.

"Oh no, I'm just here with my friend," she said. "Jemma."

"Okay, Jemma, let's be having you. Now, this is what I want you to do . . ."

"Andrew, I've made you a coffee. We need to talk."

Mr. Farrant paused from flicking through a pile of papers. "I'm rather busy," he began, seeing the determined expression on his mother-in-law's face.

WHERE DO WE GO FROM HERE?

"This won't take long," insisted Jemma's gran. "Now, about this move . . ."

"Don't you worry your head," said Mr. Farrant. "You can come and see us whenever you like and we'll phone and . . ."

"Don't patronise me!" she snapped. "I am not in the least bit worried about me. I have my Tom. It's Jemma I'm concerned for."

Andrew sighed. "So, she's been bending your ear, has she?" he said. "She's just being a typical adolescent—ignore it."

"Oh it makes me so mad when parents talk like that!" she exploded. "Jemma is not a typical anything. Jemma is Jemma. An individual. With hopes and fears and thoughts and feelings. And you are riding roughshod over all of them!"

Andrew's eyes widened. "I beg your pardon?" he said.

His mother-in-law sat down in a chair and stretched her legs. "Look, Andrew," she said, "I know this job move is a great step up and I'm very happy for you. You've worked hard and you deserve it. But you have to see it through Jemma's eyes. She is fifteen, with a great acting career ahead of her and you . . ."

"And I am making sure that she gets this stage nonsense out of her head and puts some solid A levels behind her!" he snapped. "It's a hard world out there and there are far more failed actors than successful ones."

"Quite right," agreed Jemma's gran. "But you can't dictate what she does with her own life. Have you never heard about meeting people halfway?"

Andrew sighed. "And how am I supposed to do that? Commute from Auchinchulish to Leehampton every weekend?"

"Don't be silly, dear," said his mother-in-law calmly. "What you have to do is sort things so that Jemma ends up begging to come to Scotland with you."

"You've lost me," sighed Andrew.

"I have a plan that would solve everything and keep everyone happy."

Andrew sighed. "I doubt that very much," he said.

"Will you hear me out?"

"Do I have a choice?"

"No," said Jemma's gran. "No, you don't."

The auditions were over and the girls were waiting in an anteroom for the results.

"You know," said Sumitha, "I just don't get it. I mean, how are they going to have a girl looking fat and dumpy and spotty and everything and then suddenly looking slim and stylish?"

"Make-up," said Jemma confidently. "And padding and stuff, I suppose."

Sumitha frowned. "I suppose," she said.

The door opened and Miss Ockley beckoned them all through to the rehearsal room. "Oscar's made his choices," she said. "Over to you, dear."

Oscar stood up and fingered his beard. "Difficult, difficult, difficult!" he boomed. "Great girls, great acting. But it's Jemma Farrant and Trixie Deene."

"Wow!" said Sumitha. "Well done!"

Jemma wasn't smiling.

"Excuse me," she said. "But how come there's two of us?"

"One for before and one for after," explained Oscar. "You're before, dear—great acting, those dear little sticky-out teeth, and I think we can make you look really down-at-heel—you're very versatile."

Jemma drew a deep breath.

"And then Trixie for afterwards . . . love the long

legs! And oh so thin! I'll need you both in studio a week tomorrow. Okay yah?"

"No," said Jemma.

Miss Ockley stared. Sumitha gasped. Oscar looked stunned.

"I'm sorry," she said. "But I don't want to do it."

"You don't want to do it?" gasped Oscar. "So why are you here?"

"Because I didn't know what a sexist, fattist, degrading advert you were going to make!" declared Jemma.

"Jemma!" admonished Miss Ockley.

But Jemma was in full flood. "I didn't know that you were going to try to sell a chocolate bar on the myth that it mattered whether you were plump or thin, whether your teeth stuck out or whether you had the odd spot."

"Well, I . . ."

"You're saying that to be a superstar your body matters more than you. Well, I was ill with an eating disorder last year because I believed people like you, and I don't want to be a part of anything that makes people who aren't perfect feel second-rate."

She picked up her jacket and grabbed Sumitha's arm. "Let's go," she said. "I've had enough."

✿   ✿   ✿

Open your eyes, Dad. Please open your eyes.

Henry Joseph lay immobile on the bed, the heart monitor bleeping monotonously over his head.

"Jon dear, why don't you pop home?" suggested his mother. "There's nothing you can do here and you must have lots of homework to do."

Jon sighed. What did homework matter? What did anything matter? His dad was dying, Laura was flirting with Simon—everything was going wrong all at once.

"Go on, dear—get some fresh air at least," encouraged his mother.

It was as he was ambling along the corridor that he spotted the payphone. He'd ring her. Just to hear her voice. Perhaps this Simon thing was all a big mistake—perhaps he was coming on to her and she had been trying to get rid of him. If he asked her, perhaps she'd come over and they could talk.

He picked up the receiver and fed a ten-pence piece into the machine. He dialled Laura's number.

"Ruth Turnbull speaking."

"Hi, Mrs. Turnbull, it's Jon."

"Jon dear—how's your father?"

"Bad," said Jon and his voice cracked in his

throat. He swallowed and took a deep breath. "Is Laura there?"

"She's not, I'm afraid," said Ruth. "She's gone out with—friends. Shall I get her to call you when she comes in?"

"No, it's Okay. Bye!" Jon gabbled and slammed the phone down.

He slammed his fist into the wall.

She was out with him. He knew it.

"Mind you, you've never been great with the girls . . ." His dad's words echoed in his ears. *" . . . I could always buy you a self-help book . . . show you how it should be done."*

"Oh, drop dead!"

Suddenly it was all too much. He couldn't bear it. He ran down the corridor through the double doors, into the carpark and slap-bang into someone coming the other way.

"Jon! Hey, what's up?" It was Rob. "I came to see you—I guessed you'd be seeing your dad—how's things?"

"Okay," said Jon, not meeting his eye.

"I guess they're not okay," said Rob calmly. "Is he really bad?"

Jon nodded and swallowed hard.

"That's hard," said Rob. "Want to talk about it?"

"No," said Jon. "Thanks and all that, but . . ."

"That's okay," said Rob. "Did Laura get in touch?"

"No," said Jon.

"She said she'd ring you last night," said Rob. "Maybe she missed you."

"Maybe she was snogging Simon!" shouted Jon, before he could stop himself.

"I doubt it," said Rob. "Simon's not like that."

Jon grunted. "He seemed pretty like that at the disco—and then last week he was chatting her up."

Rob leaned against the wall. "I guess you haven't heard the rumours," he said. "Maybe I shouldn't say anything, but at least I can stop you worrying. Simon's gay."

18

Moments of Truth

"So what do you think?" Sumitha was slumped, panting, on Jemma's bed, after showing her the routine for Paper Turkey's new song.

"It's amazing!" said Jemma.

"The track or my dance?"

"Both!" laughed Jemma. "Have you shown Seb and the others yet?"

Sumitha shook her head. "Right now, I'm more worried about how I'm going to get to the gig next Saturday. Not content with banning discos, my dad has put a total stop on anything that could possibly resemble fun until the exams are over. Maybe I should just drop the whole idea."

Jemma shook her head. "No way!" she said. "We have to think of something."

Jon walked slowly back into the ward. If what Rob said was really true, then he didn't have to worry about losing Laura. But if it was true, Simon would never have asked her out in the first place.

"Jon! Jon! Over here—quickly!" His mother was beckoning him frantically from the side of his father's bed and a nurse was hovering over him.

His heart rose into his throat. Please don't let anything have happened, he prayed. Please. I'll be good for ever.

"He's coming round," whispered his mother. The nurse smiled.

Henry opened his eyes. "Anona?" he said. "Jon?"

"Henry dear," said Anona and a tear trickled down her face.

"Hi, Dad," said Jon.

"Have you done your homework?" whispered Henry and closed his eyes again.

"Now, Mr. Joseph, we don't need to worry about that sort of thing," said the nurse.

But Jon smiled. The fact that his dad was worrying about just that was very comforting. He was going to get better. He knew he was.

"Jemma dear, now your friend has gone, could I have a word?" Her gran stuck her head round the bedroom door.

" 'Course—come in, Gran." Jemma shoved her books under her bed and patted the space beside her.

"Miss Ockley phoned," said her gran, who was not a woman given to beating about the bush.

"Ah," said Jemma.

"Ah indeed," said her gran. "As luck would have it, I took the call and to date have chosen not to say anything to your parents."

She broke into a grin. "I gather you gave this Oscar guy quite a dressing-down."

Jemma looked sheepish. "I suppose I was a bit rude," she admitted. "But, Gran, honestly—this advert is going to be so fattist and sexist and . . ."

She stopped.

"I suppose you know that I wasn't meant to be there," she said.

Her gran nodded. "I gather that your father thinks this stage-struck stuff has gone far enough," she said.

Jemma nodded. "But it's all I want to do!" she insisted. "I love acting—and now they're dragging me off to Scotland."

"According to your mum, you say you're not going!"

Jemma heaved a deep sigh. "I say that," she said.

"But at the end of the day what choice do I have? I can hardly stay here on my own, can I?"

"True," said her gran. "And your father is right—acting is a very precarious profession."

Jemma nodded. "So you think I should do A levels instead?"

"Not instead, as well as," said her grandmother.

Jemma frowned. "Oh, and I guess Okinwhatever is overrun with schools that do drama and A levels?"

"I doubt it very much," said her gran.

Jemma peered at her knowingly. "You," she said, "have got something up your sleeve. What is it?"

Her gran tapped the side of her nose with her finger. "All in good time," she said. "Just let me say that all is not lost—I don't want you messing up your mock exams through worrying about Scotland. Trust me?"

"Yes," said Jemma. "I trust you."

"Oh good," said her gran. "Let's have some hot chocolate and a doughnut."

19
Testing Times

Throughout the following week, everyone ate, slept, and dreamed exams. Miss McConnell, Mr. Sharpe, Toddy, and the rest of the teachers at Lee Hill made it their life's work to instil fear and trembling into their year eleven pupils. Parents pulled plugs out of TV sets and proffered cups of cocoa and useless bits of advice about deep breathing and thinking positive thoughts.

On Monday, in between the German exam from hell and science paper one, Laura finally caught up with Jon.

"How's your dad?" she said awkwardly. "I did phone but there was no reply."

"Getting better," said Jon shortly. "I rang you too. You were at Simon's."

Laura swallowed. "Yes, well, he asked me . . ."

"You shouldn't be going round with him," began Jon and then stopped. That came out all wrong. "I

mean, he's not right for you—he's . . ."

"Oh isn't he?" snapped Laura, who was feeling pretty guilty as it was. "And you know just what is right for me, do you?"

"I thought I was," said Jon.

Laura felt mean. "I like you a lot," she said. "But that doesn't stop me having other friends."

"Is that what he is? Just a friend?"

"Of course," said Laura. "I've said so, haven't I?"

But Jon didn't feel she said it with much conviction.

On Tuesday, Miss McConnell told Chelsea that her sociology essay had been her best piece of work ever.

"I've always known you were bright," she said, "but this was exceptional. I loved the angle you took—where did you get such a feel for the subject?"

"My dad lost his job a couple of years back, my mum's out of work now and giving me hell and . . ."

"Your mother? Out of work?" Miss McConnell sounded as surprised as if Chelsea had declared that the Queen had part-time work in Safeways.

"The radio job folded," said Chelsea. "She's looking for something new."

"Is she now?" said Miss McConnell. "How fascinating."

It was, thought Chelsea, amazing what interested some people.

"Good luck with the sociology paper this afternoon," said Miss McConnell. "I think you should seriously think about doing it at A level."

It was something Chelsea had never even considered.

By Wednesday, Sumitha was mega worried. The guys had thought her routine was ace and she had assured them that she would be at the leisure centre at seven P.M. on Saturday. But the nearer it got, the more she panicked. She couldn't just walk out of the house and not tell anyone where she was going. But telling them was just as impossible.

Maybe she'd back out of it. After all, it wasn't worth messing up at home—not just for one gig.

She'd phone Seb now, before school, and tell him. He'd be pretty put out about it, but there was no choice.

She dragged herself downstairs to the phone but, just as she was about to lift the receiver, it rang.

"Hello? Sumitha Banerji speaking."

"Sumitha? This is your cousin's neighbour Sajjed here. From Sheffield. And how are you?"

"Very well, thank you," she replied politely.

"So pleased we are that we are all to meet very soon," said the voice. "And Asim will be so happy to get to know you and . . ."

The conversation blurred. This was the guy her father had been writing to. So her mother had let the letter go. After all Sumitha had said. She felt a red-hot anger rising up inside her.

"Sumitha? Who is on the phone?"

Her father stuck his head round the kitchen door.

"It's for you!" snapped Sumitha. She thrust the receiver at him and stamped back upstairs.

"A delight indeed!" she heard her father say. "Of course, of course. Please—any time over the next few days that suits you. We shall be so very happy. Oh yes, and Sumitha too."

That did it.

She stormed downstairs and into the kitchen, where her father was regaling her mother with details of the conversation.

"We shall not be happy!" she stormed. "I know just who that was and you are not going to do this to me."

Her father turned in amazement.

"You are such a total hypocrite!" she shouted. "One minute you are nagging at me to work, work, work for my future and the next you are organising that future for me!"

"Sumitha!" her mother exclaimed. "Apologise to your father!"

"What for?" she shouted. "Wanting a say in my own life?"

Her father's eyes narrowed and his lips formed into a stern, thin line. "I want only the best for you . . ." he began.

"Get real!" shouted Sumitha. "You don't know what's best for me—you don't even know me at all!" And, with that, she grabbed her lunch box and wrenched open the back door

"Sumitha, your breakfast!" began her mother. "You can't do exams on an empty stomach."

"Stuff breakfast, stuff exams," said Sumitha. "Stuff everything."

"Sumitha! Wait!"

Chelsea hurtled across the school yard towards her friend. She had a physics exam in twenty minutes and she couldn't remember anything about conduction. Sumitha would know it all, Sumitha knew everything.

"Hey, Sumitha—you know conduction . . . ? Hey, what's the matter?"

Sumitha was crying. "I'm fine," she said.

"No you're not," said Chelsea, taking her arm. "Tell me. Maybe I can help."

Sumitha's face crumpled. "Why won't they let me do anything that you lot do? Anything at all? Why?"

"So you see," said Sumitha, ten minutes and half a packet of tissues later, "I just don't know what to do. Half of me wants to do what's going to keep the peace because I love them, and the other half of me thinks that if I'm going to have to live by their outmoded rules for the rest of my life, I need to grab at all the fun while I can."

Chelsea nodded. "It must be really hard for you," she agreed. "I can't imagine it. But surely, not all Hindu people have arranged marriages?"

Sumitha shook her head. "Fewer and fewer," she said. "And deep down, I know that my dad wouldn't make me marry anyone I didn't like—it's just the whole awful business of meeting people, knowing that they are sizing you up, deciding whether you are worthy of their precious son."

Chelsea nodded. "Well, if you're going to do the Battle of the Bands, we need a plan."

"We?"

"Oh yes," said Chelsea confidently. "The more people involved, the easier to cover our tracks."

"But what can I say?" pleaded Sumitha.

Chelsea thought for a moment. "The secret," she said, "is to tell the truth for as long as possible. Too many lies and it gets complicated. So, we say you're going to the leisure centre."

"We WHAT?" exploded Sumitha. "Telling them about the gig is a sure fire way of having them lock me in for the duration."

"Did I say anything about the gig?" questioned Chelsea. "It's at the leisure centre, isn't it? So we say that's where we are going. They'll assume we are going to play badminton or sit in the coffee shop or something."

Sumitha eyed her with admiration. "That's brilliant!" she breathed. "But what if Dad says I have to stay in?"

"He won't," said Chelsea. "Not if you do as I say."

❀ ❀ ❀

"Gran has something to tell you," said Jemma's mother over supper on Wednesday evening. "Mother?"

Jemma's grandmother laid down her knife and fork. "I think," she said, "I have a solution to your problem. When your mum and dad move to Scotland, why don't you come and live with Tom and me? Just in term-time, of course. While you're at drama school. And you can fly to Scotland for the holidays."

Jemma's eyes widened.

"Gran, that would be brilliant!" she said. "But Dad said I couldn't go to drama school." She threw her father a withering look.

"As long as you agree to take A levels as well," said her father, "just so you have something to fall back on, I suppose I'll have to put up with it."

Jemma leaped up and flung her arms round his neck. "Thanks, Dad. I'll make you proud of me, I promise. When I'm a mega famous film star, you won't regret it."

It was after Jemma had hurtled out to phone her friends with the news that Jemma's gran patted Claire's arm and smiled. "Don't look so devastated," she said.

"How do you expect me to look?" moaned Claire. "She jumped at the idea—how will I cope without her?"

"You won't have to," said her mother assertively.

Claire frowned. "Mother, what are you on about?"

"I think," said Andrew, pouring out the coffee, "that we should let things take their course. Your mother has a plan."

"Not another one," sighed Claire.

"A winner," said her mother.

"We need to talk," said Jon's mother on Thursday. "Now your father is getting better, we need to make plans. He can't go back to that job, you know."

Jon nodded.

"So, will you go to Cornwall?"

His mother shook her head. "Not right now," she said.

"But, Mum, if it's the only way he'll be happy, you have to go. I mean, you can't let him get ill again."

"Hang on a minute," she said. "Just hear me out. If I give up everything I'm doing and go to Cornwall right now, I'll be fed up and grumpy and that won't help our marriage. It does need help, Jon," she added softly.

Jon said nothing.

"And, besides, you've another year at school and I've got a college course to finish."

"And, meanwhile, Dad gets ill again!" shouted Jon.

"Meanwhile, Dad retires, takes it easy, recuperates—and then, when you leave school, we go to Cornwall. I hear St. Ives is very arty—I might open a design consultancy there."

Jon beamed. "So you did listen to Dad!" he exclaimed. "You have thought about it."

"A lot," said Anona. "Once you're at art college it won't matter so much where we live—but right now, leaving you behind would give me a heart attack!"

It was the first time his mum had cracked a joke since his dad had been ill. Things were getting better.

If only it wasn't for Laura.

"Sumitha? It's Seb."

Sumitha's heart lurched.

"Look, Tate's got a sore throat so we've cancelled the practice. Can you bear to just come along on

Saturday and do your routine? Tate daren't risk his voice going."

"Fine!" said Sumitha with relief. "It'll save me thinking of yet another excuse."

"Do you want a lift?"

"I think," said Sumitha, "that if you drove up to my house in your roadster, my father would have a seizure. I'll meet you there."

"What will you wear to the gig?" asked Jemma on Friday morning.

"I've thought of that," said Sumitha proudly. "I've got to look mega boring when we go out, so I'll wear my old school mac, knee-high boots, and black gloves."

Laura pulled a face. "That's hardly going to set the band alight."

"No, but underneath—well, wait and see."

Sumitha grinned. "If I'm going to do this, I might as well go the whole way."

"What's this?" said Jemma at tea-time, prodding a lump of colourless food.

"Gran's special recipe that she brought back from China," said her mother. "It's rice and bean-sprouts and fish and seaweed and . . ."

"Can I have beans on toast?" said Jemma.

"But, darling," said her grandmother, "don't you think foreign food is so much more fun?"

If Chelsea hadn't stayed late to work in the library, she would never have known. But when the peace of the study area was shattered by the sound of breaking glass in the yard outside, and Miss Maddox, the librarian, had rushed to the window to see the cause of the commotion, it had been Chelsea who had spotted the small, wiry figure pushing through the gap in the hedge beside the bike-sheds. Two bigger boys vaulted the hedge and ran off in the opposite direction.

"Who is that child?" demanded Miss Maddox, gesturing in the direction of the small kid.

"I don't know, Miss," Chelsea assured her.

But she did.

It was Ricky.

"Bex? It's Chelsea. Listen, this is urgent. Ricky's in trouble."

Chelsea was only halfway through the story when the pips went. "I've no more money," she

210

said, rummaging in her pockets in desperation.

"I'll come home," said Bex. "I'll be back by lunch-time tomorrow. I'll call you."

"Okay," said Chelsea.

"And, Chelsea?"

"Yes?"

"Thanks."

When Chelsea got home, her mum was sitting in front of the television with a cheese roll and a miserable expression.

"Before you ask, I am, apparently, not model material," said Ginny.

I never thought you were, thought Chelsea. "Never mind," she said cheerfully. "Why don't you just stick with writing? That's what you're good at, after all."

"Oh yes," said her mother. "So good that newspapers up and down the country are falling over themselves to employ me. The irony of it is that I've spent years solving other people's problems and now I can't even solve my own."

"But you could solve mine," said Chelsea. "Please?"

Ginny inclined her head. "Tell me," she said.

Chelsea told her.

"So you didn't actually see Ricky throw whatever it was that broke the window?" said her mother.

Chelsea shook her head. "I just recognised him as he ran off—and there were two other, older guys involved too."

Ginny nodded. "So maybe he wasn't guilty. And you did well to phone Bex. You'll work out what to do."

"ME?"

Her mother nodded. "I get the feeling you are quite good at this sort of thing."

20
Courage to the Fore

"Dad?" Sumitha said, on Saturday morning, taking a deep breath and putting on her fondest expression. "Would it be all right for me to go to the leisure centre for a couple of hours this evening? We thought a game of badminton would cheer up Jon."

"What a good idea!" interrupted her mother swiftly. "Exercise is just the thing for clearing the head after study. And so kind to think of poor Jon. Is it not, Rajiv?"

Sumitha held her breath.

"The leisure centre, you say?"

Sumitha nodded and held her breath some more.

"You may," said her father. "But you must be home by ten thirty."

Sumitha gasped. That was far too early. But she wasn't stupid enough to argue.

"Thanks, Dad, you're a superstar!" she said.

And thought how much nicer her father looked when he grinned.

"It's okay! It worked."

Sumitha put her mouth close to the receiver and whispered down the phone to Chelsea. "Can you sort the others?"

"Leave it to me," said Chelsea.

"Jon? It's Chelsea here. How's your dad? Really? Oh I am glad. Listen, we all want you to come out with us tonight."

"All of you?" Jon had said it before he thought.

Chelsea knew just what he was getting at. "Yes—Laura would have phoned, only she's had to go out with her mum," she lied. "But, listen, it's kind of top secret. This is the plan . . ."

"So, are you up for it?" Chelsea asked Laura.

"Sure," said Laura. "I'll even wear trainers to make it look authentic. I'll tell Simon."

"Laura, you're not going to bring Simon, surely?" protested Chelsea.

"Of course," said Laura. "Why not?"

She certainly wasn't going to miss the opportunity to get Simon on to the dance floor, and hopefully lure him into a few passionate kisses.

Chelsea took a deep breath. "Because you're supposed to be Jon's girlfriend," she said.

"Not for much longer," said Laura.

"So has Simon . . . ? I mean, do you and Simon . . . ?" Chelsea's voice trailed off. She didn't know how to get round to it.

"Honestly!" shouted Laura. "What is it with you lot? Simon's a really nice, gentle, caring guy. I like him a lot."

"I know," said Chelsea. "But so is Jon. And he likes you a lot."

"Well," snapped Laura, "if you're so mad keen on Jon, you go out with him!" And she slammed down the phone.

"Jemma, darling, don't you think you should tidy this bedroom for Mum?"

Jemma's gran was peering round the door and turning up her nose at the debris scattered over the carpet.

"Later, Gran, I'm revising," said Jemma.

"What are you doing?" asked her gran, plonking herself down on the bed. "Do tell me."

Jemma sighed. She had far too much to get through to start explaining velocity to her grandmother. "This and that—look, Gran, I really must . . ."

"I don't think that sweater is quite your colour, sweetheart," her grandmother went on. "I always liked you in yellow myself."

"Yellow is out!" hissed Jemma. "Please, Gran, I must work—or I won't get this done before tonight."

"Oh yes, tonight. I hear Dad said you could stay out till late—I don't think I approve of that. Not in the middle of exams. And you hear such stories . . ."

"GRAN!" Jemma closed her eyes and sent up a silent prayer. She was seeing a side to her gran that she had never noticed before. And she didn't much like it.

Jon wasn't sure that he really wanted to go to this gig. He knew it was really cool of his mates to rally round, but Laura still hadn't phoned and he was sure that if she wanted to be with him, she would have done. She was friendly enough at school, but every time he asked to see her, she made some excuse about revision or homework, neither of which had ever bothered her much in the past. He knew she was going to dump him. Maybe he should get in first.

But if what Rob said was right, there couldn't be anything between Simon and Laura. He wished he knew. In fact, he had to know. He would make it his business to find out.

And there was only one way to do that.

"Chelsea? It's me, Bex. I don't suppose you know where Ricky is?"

Chelsea frowned at the telephone. "No—isn't he at home?"

"I just got here and the place is empty. Don't worry—I'll go hunting for him. But if you see him around town, tell him I'm back. Okay?"

"Sure," said Chelsea. "And, Bex?"

"Yes?"

"Don't worry. We'll sort it."

"Is Simon in? I'm a mate of his from school."

Jon prayed that he wasn't going to make a total fool of himself.

"Si! Someone to see you!"

Simon clattered down the stairs and stopped dead when he saw Jon.

"I wanted to have a chat with you," said Jon in a rush. "There's something I need to know."

Simon swallowed and grabbed a jacket off a peg in the hall. "I thought you might," he said. "Let's go for a walk."

He slammed the front door behind them. "It's about Laura, isn't it?" he said.

Jon nodded. "Look—this is difficult, but well, I really like Laura and I thought she liked me, but now it seems you two are an item and she hardly speaks to me and well, I've heard rumours."

Simon stared at him. "What rumours?" he whispered.

"You have to tell me what's going on," said Jon. "Is it true that you're gay?"

"So you see," said Simon, "I can't answer you. I mean, I don't know. I guess maybe I am."

Jon frowned. "But you came on strong to Laura . . ."

Simon shook his head. "I've been an absolute dork about that," he said. "You see, my dad and my sister have been going on and on at me for ages, about never getting a girlfriend and liking cooking and hating sport—and they've kept making hints

218

about me liking guys more than girls and I got sick of it."

Jon nodded. "I can see that," he said.

"So I thought that if I went out with a girl, and took her home to meet them, they'd shut up and leave me alone. It's pretty tough when your family want you to be something you can't be. Not that I'd expect you to understand."

"Oh, I understand," said Jon. "Believe me, I understand. But you can't lead Laura on—I mean, sadly, I think she likes you. She thinks it's going somewhere."

Simon nodded. "I'll tell her tonight," he said. "I'm really sorry, Jon. You will be there, won't you? To pick up the pieces?"

"Try stopping me," said Jon. "And, Simon?"

"Yes?"

"I reckon that's a really brave thing you've just done. Thanks, mate."

Step Kick and Change

"**W**e've done it!" breathed Sumitha in disbelief. "We're here!"

The main hall of the leisure centre had been transformed, with huge gantries of overhead lights, a massive central stage, and two enormous video screens.

"I must go and find the guys," said Sumitha. "Wish me luck!"

"Break a leg!" said Jemma.

"Pardon?"

"That's the way we stage people say good luck," said Jemma.

"Weird," said Sumitha.

"So you came!" Seb grinned at Sumitha. "Tate said you would chicken out."

"As if," said Sumitha, who so nearly had. "Are you okay?"

Seb's cheeks were flushed and he was hopping from one foot to the other.

He leaned towards her and kissed her cheek. "Never better, babe!"

He smelled foul. Sumitha drew back in disgust. His breath smelled of cheap beer, and his movements were clumsy.

"Let's see the costume," said Tate, greasing back his hair with the palms of his hands.

Sumitha showed him.

"Wowee!" said Tate.

"Sex-eeeee," said Seb. "See me after!" Which should have pleased Sumitha.

Only it didn't. It made her feel very uncomfortable. And suddenly she began to wonder whether all this hadn't been one very big mistake.

"Have you told her yet?" Jon asked Simon, as everyone surged forward to hear the first band.

Simon shook his head. "I'm trying to find the right moment," he said. "It's so noisy in here."

"Just do it," said Jon.

"Right," said Simon.

❀   ❀   ❀

The first band, Cookies 'n Cream, were really loud but not much good and the second, Coincidence, were so eighties, it wasn't true. Then Living Daylights did a really cool, smoochy number. Laura slipped her hand into Simon's. He slipped it away.

"Laura," he muttered. "Can you come outside for a minute? I want to tell you something."

This is it, thought Laura. He's going to admit he loves me. And that he's too shy to kiss me here, but he can't wait.

"Of course," she said, flicking a finger through her hair. "Of course I'll come."

"You are WHAT?" Laura stared, open-mouthed, at Simon, who had flushed a bright shade of red.

"I think I'm gay," he repeated. "I'm sorry, Laura, really I'm sorry."

He laid a hand on her shoulder.

"Get away from me!" she shouted, pushing him off. "You disgust me! I thought you loved me and all the time . . . How could you?"

"I didn't mean to hurt you," Simon blurted out. "I really thought that with you it could be different.

I mean, I really, really like you and I hoped I'd feel, well, you know . . ."

"What? Normal, you mean? Well, you didn't, did you?" Tears began running down Laura's cheeks.

"You just used me!" she sobbed. "Well, thanks. Thanks a million!" She turned and walked away.

"Laura! Laura, come back! Where are you going? The band's on in a minute."

"So you go and listen to the stupid band, then!" she cried. "Just leave me alone."

"And now it's band number five—Paper Turkey!"

Everyone broke into applause and then laughed as Sumitha came on stage in her old school mac and knee-high boots, with a battered brown Derby hat on her head.

"What is she doing?" gasped Chelsea. "I thought she was only wearing the mac to cover up her costume from her dad. What's with the hat?"

"Wait and see," said Jemma.

The band struck up and Sumitha began dancing. As she ripped off her mac and hat, the audience erupted into cheers and wolf whistles. Underneath, she was wearing very short, very sparkly hot pants in bright purple and a halter-neck top in shocking pink. She had pulled her hair high up on her head in a ponytail, fastened with a spangled scrunchie.

As she began to dance, the noise subsided. Everyone was enthralled as she began breakdancing, clicking her fingers, doing foot rolls, step kicks, jump splits and knee hops. The band picked up the body movement, rolling their shoulders and thrusting their hips.

"She's brill!" said Jemma.

"Incredible," agreed Chelsea. "She doesn't look too happy, though."

"Where's Laura?" said Jon.

At the end of the song, Sumitha did two cartwheels across the stage and on the final drumbeat she did the splits, throwing her arms wide open to the audience.

The cheers went on for ages. Foot stamping, clapping and shouts of "Wicked!" and "More!" reverberated around the hall.

Sumitha ran off the stage and grabbed her things.

"You were brill!" said Seb, enveloping her in a hug. Sumitha shrugged him off. "Hey, what's with the cold shoulder? This is a time for celebrating."

"I have to go," said Sumitha.

"You have to what? Get real!"

Sumitha nibbled her lip. She just wanted to get out of there. She felt cheap and tacky. She suddenly saw herself through her father's eyes. She was a good dancer, she knew that. But when she had been on stage, and seen all the guys ogling her and calling out risqué comments, she had wanted to disappear. She didn't want just anyone seeing her like that. Only someone really special. And, right now, there wasn't anyone special. Not even Seb.

"It was fun," she said. "Thanks. But I really have to go. Let me know if you win. And if you do, leave off the drink—you weren't half so good tonight."

She took some satisfaction from the gobsmacked looks on the faces of the three boys.

"Sumitha! You were great!"

"Well done!"

"How did it feel?"

Sumitha looked at her friends. "Awful," she said softly. "I wish I had never come."

"But you did so well," began Jemma.

Sumitha shook her head. "It's not me," she said. "The dancing is great—but not like this. I can't explain." She felt her eyes fill with tears.

"Do you want to go home now?" said Chelsea gently, taking her arm. "I can always ring my mum and get her to come round early."

Sumitha was about to agree when Jon rushed up to them, looking very worried. "I can't find Laura anywhere," he said. "Simon—Simon told her he was gay. She's gone. What shall I do?"

"Don't worry," said Chelsea at once. "We'll find her."

"Rushing around like this isn't going to do any good," said Jon, after they had belted round the carpark, up to the squash courts and down to the gym. "What do people do when they're miserable?"

"Cry?" offered Sumitha, who wanted to.

"Eat chocolate," said Jemma.

"Jemma," said Chelsea, "you're a star. You do the swimming-pool area, I'll look by the badminton courts."

Chelsea found her, sitting by the chocolate machine in the ladies' changing-rooms, sniffing miserably.

"Hey, Laura, don't cry," said Chelsea. "It's not the end of the world."

Laura wiped a hand across her eyes. "You know?"

Chelsea nodded.

"I feel so—used," sobbed Laura. "And it's so—disgusting."

Chelsea looked rather stern. "No, it's not," she said. "Whether Simon is or isn't gay—and even he's not sure—doesn't alter the kind of guy he is. He's really interested in what you do, he's got a wicked sense of humour . . ."

"I know all that!" snapped Laura. "That's why I love him. And all the time he was just pretending to want to go out with me. He didn't fancy me at all. How could he?"

"He didn't mean it," said Chelsea. "Jon says that his dad was being really cruel and I guess he just wanted to try to seem like all his mates."

Laura looked up. "Jon knew? About Simon?"

"He only found out today," said Chelsea hastily. "He'd heard rumours and he couldn't bear to think of you getting hurt, so he asked Simon right out."

Laura stared at her. "Really? He didn't want me hurt? After what I did to him?"

She sighed. "I've been so selfish," she said. "He'll never forgive me."

"I bet he will," said Chelsea. "But there's only one way to find out. Go and ask him. He's outside in the . . ."

But Laura had already gone.

"Jon's taking me home in a taxi," said Laura proudly. "We want to be alone. Will you tell your mum?"

Chelsea nodded. "Good luck," she said. "Jon does love you, really he does."

"I know," said Laura.

"And you?"

"I honestly don't know," she said. "But I think I've got a lot of making up to do."

"So how was the concert?" Mrs. Gee opened the passenger door and the gang piled in.

"Ace," said Chelsea. And stopped. "That is to say we went to play . . ."

"Come off it," grinned Ginny, switching on the ignition and putting the car into gear. "I wasn't born yesterday."

"You haven't said . . ." began Sumitha.

"I haven't said a word to anyone," Ginny assured her, turning out on to the main road. "But I do

228

rather think, dear, that your father might wonder why you need a sequin scrunchie and that rather fetching top for a serious evening of sport."

Sumitha pulled her mac tighter around her and tied the belt.

"Look, Sumitha," said Ginny, "I know what you were doing."

Sumitha blanched.

"The guy at the *Echo* who was going to write up the gig was taken ill with food poisoning. The editor had this silly idea of getting an old geriatric like me to go along and write a funny piece about being bewildered by modern music. So I came. You dance well, Sumitha."

It was all too much. Sumitha knew she'd done wrong. She knew she would never be so stupid again. But for Chelsea's mum to find out—and obviously tell her father—was just too much. She burst into tears.

"My dear child, don't cry," said Ginny, passing her a tissue from the glove compartment. "You don't think I am going to say anything, do you? I was young once, myself, you know. And there's been no harm done. This time."

Sumitha sniffed. "I feel so tacky," she said. "It was

all a big mistake. My dad's right—not everything my mates do is right for me."

"Well," said Ginny, turning into Sumitha's road, "be honest—tell him just that. He'll be a very proud man."

She pulled up outside Sumitha's house.

Lights were blazing in all the downstairs rooms and on the driveway was a dark blue Mercedes, parked beside Rajiv's Volvo.

"It would appear you have visitors," said Ginny.

Sumitha gulped.

"It's Sajjed. I can't go in," she gasped. "They'll introduce me and I'll take my coat off and . . ."

The tears began again. "What am I going to do?"

Ginny shook her head. "It looks, dear, as if you will have to face the music," she said.

Chelsea grabbed her mother's arm. "Mum," she said. "Are you really on Sumitha's side? I mean, truly and properly."

"I don't take sides about things I don't understand," said Ginny hastily. "But I don't want to see her in more trouble."

"Right," said Chelsea. "Leave it to me. This is what we do."

❀ ❀ ❀

"Any moment now, she will be home," smiled Rajiv to his visitors. "She is an obedient child, and respects my rules."

"Which is indeed as it should be," agreed Sajjed, nibbling a samosa and eyeing the room with interest. "Our Asim is the same."

His son glared at him and looked at the floor.

"Such a pretty home you have," murmured Chhobi, Asim's mother.

Chitrita, who felt that the general interest in her personal possessions went beyond ordinary politeness, stood up. "Some more tea?" she enquired. "Or a little . . . oh my goodness, what is that?"

The screech of a car alarm shattered the peace of the room.

"My car!" shouted Sajjed and ran to the door. "Come, Asim!"

Rajiv, Chitrita, and Chhobi followed anxiously.

"I do hope it has not been damaged," whispered Rajiv to his wife. "It would give a very bad impression of our neighbourhood."

They all rushed out into the garden.

"Oh, Mr. Banerji," cried Ginny Gee, grabbing

his arm and holding on to it firmly. "Your car—I believe someone was tampering with it as we drove up."

"It is not his—it is mine!" said Sajjed. "A most expensive vehicle!"

He walked all round his car, touching it fondly. "It seems all right. Thank heaven."

"No harm done then," said Ginny, still holding Rajiv's arm.

"So kind of you to bring Sumitha home," said Chitrita. "Where is she?"

Chelsea smiled her sweetest smile. "She's gone inside, Mrs. Banerji. She knew you would be anxious."

Rajiv beamed. "You see?" he said to his guest. "Such a reliable girl."

He led them all inside.

"That," said Ginny with a grin, to her daughter, "was a piece of very quick thinking."

Upstairs, in the bathroom, with the door firmly locked, Sumitha stripped off her hot pants and stepped into her *salwar kameez*.

Her dad was probably right in most of what he said—but she was glad that Chelsea had a mum who wasn't quite such a stickler for the truth. And

232

she was lucky to have such a smart friend, with a very good line in bouncing on car bumpers.

"And this is Asim," said Rajiv. "Asim, this is my daughter, Sumitha."

Sumitha tried to look withdrawn and sullen, but when she looked at Asim's smiling face and dancing black eyes, she couldn't help smiling herself.

"So good for these young people to start to know one another," said Sajjed.

"Indeed," said Rajiv. "Who knows where it may lead?"

Sumitha closed her eyes. How could he do this? So blatantly?

Asim took a deep breath. "I think I should speak," he said. "I can't do this."

Nobody moved.

Sumitha opened her eyes and looked at him in astonishment.

"I think Sumitha is very pretty, and I am sure that this is a delightful family. But I cannot just let you all assume that I will get to know your daughter and then maybe, in a few years, marry her. I know it is tradition—but I cannot be part of it. My world is different from yours, please see that. I have to live my life my way."

Sumitha looked at him with admiration. She knew just how hard it must have been to say that. She had a fair idea of what sort of family argument would follow when he got home.

The two men both opened their mouths to speak, but Chitrita got in first. "Asim, I think what you have said is very sensible." She threw a nervous glance at Rajiv and took a deep breath. "We wanted to bring our children up in England, so how can we blame them when they want to adopt at least some of the English ways?"

"It is so," agreed Chhobi. "I am sorry, Sajjed, but I must have my say also. Asim is a young man with many ambitions. He wants to travel, to see the world. He will meet many young women and in his own time fall in love."

"But that is so often the route to disaster!" exclaimed Rajiv.

"Indeed so!" agreed Sajjed.

"True," said Chitrita. "But these young people have to choose their own road and follow where it leads. We cannot live their lives for them."

"Where are they, anyway?" asked Chhobi, turning and looking round the room.

In the kitchen, Sumitha poured a glass of cola and smiled at Asim. "Thanks," she said.

"What for?" said Asim.

"Saying what I was thinking," said Sumitha.

Asim smiled. "So you were not offended?"

"Offended?" said Sumitha. "I have never been more relieved in my life."

"We could, of course, still keep in touch," suggested Asim. "See one another occasionally. If you'd like, that is."

"I think that would be great," smiled Sumitha. "After all, good daughters always do what their fathers want, don't they?"

Chitrita was amazed when she came into the kitchen to make more tea, to find Sumitha and Asim doubled up with laughter.

22
The Way Forward

"**M**um, you were mega!" said Chelsea, giving her a hug. "No one else's mum would be so cool."

Ginny grinned. "One likes to be of service," she teased. "By the way, Bex phoned while you were out. She said to tell you that she found Ricky hanging out with two guys from their estate. Apparently they had been threatening him and taking cash—the whole bit. She's had a long chat with him and he's going to tell the headmaster everything on Monday."

Chelsea sighed with relief. "Thank goodness," she said. "You don't think Mr. Todd will be too hard on him, do you? I mean, he's had a rough deal at home and everything. His mum hits him, you know."

Ginny sighed. "That's terrible," she said. "And way out of our league."

"Surely, you of all people know what to do," said Chelsea. "You talk—talked—to people about their problems every day."

"A chat show is one thing," said her mum. "But you can't just blunder into sorting out other people's lives."

"Well, I reckon there must be loads of kids who need someone like you," said Chelsea. "I know, you could write books—you know, about divorce and domestic violence and what to do when you are bullied and stuff."

Ginny said nothing.

"Mum?"

"Do you know," said Ginny softly, "I do believe I could. Would kids read them?"

"Of course they would!" exclaimed Chelsea. "You've no idea how hard growing up can be. There aren't any signposts."

"That's it! Chelsea, you're amazing!"

"Pardon?"

"Signposts—a whole series of books called the 'Signpost Series.' Signposts to solving shyness, Signposts to dealing with grief—Chelsea, you've just sorted my career!"

"Oh good—I wish I could sort mine," said

Chelsea. "What can you do with sociology?"

"All sorts," said Ginny. "Probation work, police force, social services . . ."

"Like helping kids like Ricky?" said Chelsea. "And sorting out problems?"

Her mother nodded.

"Oh good," said Chelsea. "In that case I'd better spend the next few months working flat out. I'm staying on for A levels."

Her mother gave her a big hug. "You might end up just like me," she said proudly.

"I think perhaps not," said Chelsea. "Have we got any biscuits?"

Jemma picked up the booklet that was on her pillow.

She flicked through the pages. This was something else. You could do absolutely any-thing—drama, singing, dance, mime, produc-

The Central Scotland School of Dramatic Art

PROSPECTUS

tion, stage management—the list was endless.

And you could do A levels. Well, Highers was

what they called them but it amounted to the same thing. There was a whole range, including theatre studies and English, which were the two she fancied most.

She peered on the back page to find the address. It was in Aberdeen. Dad had said that Auchinchulish was about three-quarters of an hour from Aberdeen. So she could go with them, and do drama, and keep him quiet by running in a couple of A levels on the side.

What's more, it would be the perfect excuse for not having to live with Gran in term-time. She adored her grandmother and it had seemed like a good idea at the time, but this had been the first visit when Gran had taken over the cooking, and the thought of weeks and weeks of that was more than Jemma could bear. Besides, she was such a stickler for tidiness and she kept wanting to know what was going on. Mum was seriously neurotic, but Jemma could handle her. Gran was a different thing altogether.

She'd show Dad the brochure in the morning and tell him he was right. That was always the best tack with adults. Lull them into a false sense of security.

It was as she was dropping off to sleep that she wondered, just fleetingly, who put the prospectus on her bed in the first place.

23
Bright Horizons

"It's so good to be home," said Jon's dad the following morning, after Anona had settled him in a chair with *Golfer's World* and a cup of decaffeinated coffee. "You know, I feel as if today is the first day of the rest of my life."

"It is," smiled his wife.

Henry patted her hand. "And I'm sorry about the Cornwall business—silly nonsense, really . . ."

"No it's not!" interjected Jon. "We're going."

Henry looked at him in amazement.

"But . . ."

"No buts, Henry," said Anona. "It's all decided. We're going as soon as Jon's finished school."

Henry's face lit up. "Really? But your design work—I was being selfish—I know that now. We don't need . . ."

"Henry! Will you just shut up and listen? I've looked into it—St. Ives is very arty—Jon would love it—and I plan to set up a design consultancy: transforming run-down cottages into upmarket weekend homes, that sort of thing."

Henry took her hand. "Really?"

"Really," said Anona. "And you can have your smallholding. But just promise me one thing."

"Anything!" said Henry cheerfully.

"I don't ever have to milk a goat or plant a carrot?"

"I promise!" Henry roared with laughter. The old, booming guffaw that Jon used to find so irritating.

Only now it sounded good. Very good indeed.

"Sumitha? It's Seb. We didn't win."

Sumitha clutched the receiver and dropped her voice. "Bad luck!" she said.

"Don't bad luck me!" said Seb. "It's your fault."

"How do you make that out?" retorted Sumitha.

Seb coughed. "One of the judges overheard your oh-so-stuffy remark about drink and disqualified us! And we had only had a few cans."

Sumitha took a deep breath. "A few too many!" she said. And put the phone down.

She was relieved. It was over.

✿   ✿   ✿

"Sumitha? Who was on the telephone?" her father asked, as Sumitha went into the sitting-room.

"Oh, just a mate from school," she said hastily.

He grinned at her. "Just wondered," he said. "There was a phone call for you earlier, while you were still asleep, but I didn't want to bother you."

"Who was it?"

"Asim," said her father. "But of course, I said you didn't want to get involved and asked him not to call again."

"Did he leave a number?"

"Yes, but . . ."

"Give it to me, Dad! Now!"

After she had hurtled to the phone, Rajiv smiled at Chitrita. "Perhaps," he said, "I've done one thing right after all."

It seemed to Jemma that Sunday lunch was as good a time as any to get things sorted once and for all.

"Dad," she said, after they had ploughed their way through what Gran called apple turnover, but what resembled a small, burnt offering, "about college?"

"Yes, dear?" said her father, dabbing his mouth

with his table napkin.

"There's this place in Aberdeen where I could do A levels *and* drama."

"There is?"

"Yes, and I've got the brochure and it looks really cool . . ."

Her mother spooned custard on to Luke's plate and removed Daniel's thumb from the remains of the turnover. "But, sweetheart, I thought you were going to stay with Gran because you didn't want to come with us?"

Jemma bit her lip. "Well, you see, I thought . . . I mean, it's not really fair on Gran, and I would miss you all and this college looks mega cool. You don't mind too much, do you, Gran?"

Her grandmother burst out laughing. "I'd have minded a whole heap more if you'd actually arrived," she laughed. "Why do you think I've done the cooking all week? And nagged you about untidy bedrooms and late nights!"

Jemma stared at her. "You set me up," she said softly.

" 'Fraid so," admitted her gran. "Don't go mad."

But far from making her angry, it made her feel very safe. And very loved.

"Thank heavens you're coming, sweetheart," said her mother, giving her a big hug. "I would have missed you so much."

"Me too," grinned Jemma.

Growing up and doing her own thing would be great. But only in easy stages.

"Laura! I didn't expect to see you again."

Simon stood back to let her into the hall.

Laura shook her head. "I won't come in," she said. "It's just—well, I'm sorry I said what I did. I was just upset and angry, I didn't mean it."

Simon grinned. "That's okay," he said. "I'm pretty mixed up about it myself. I suppose the old cliché about still being friends is out of the question, is it?"

Laura grinned back. "I always did like the old clichés the best," she said. "And, besides, who else can I read poetry with?"

"Isn't it wonderful?" said Laura, a week later, as they all sat on the art-block steps during the lunch hour. "You work yourself into a stupor, pass all the wretched mocks, and then get a lecture from Miss McConnell about not taking success for granted and pushing on to ever greater heights. Can't they ever just say 'well done'?"

Chelsea pulled a face. "At least you passed all yours—I got nagged like crazy about it being no good getting As in sociology and English if I couldn't pass maths. But I will, even if it means taking those extra classes old Toddy keeps offering me."

Jemma grinned. "You've gone very dedicated all of a sudden," she said.

"There's a point to it all now," replied Chelsea. "For the first time ever, I know where I'm going and what I'm going to do. It's such a relief."

Jemma nodded. "It must be," she said. "I can't say I'm smitten with this Scotland idea, but at least I get to do drama. And much as I hate to admit it, Dad does have a point. If I don't make it as an actress, I can be a stage manager, or even teach drama."

"It'll be weird without you," said Chelsea. "But at least us three will be together."

"I might not be," said Sumitha quietly.

The others stared at her.

"How come?" demanded Chelsea. "You're the brightest of all of us."

"My dad's offered to send me to Keene College," she said.

"But that's an all-girls' school," said Laura in disgust. "You'd hate it."

Sumitha grinned.

"I'd love it," she said. "I don't have a clue what I want to do when I leave school, but I do know that I want to be independent, to have a career, and not to end up just getting married for the sake of it, like so many of my Bengali friends. I want to be able to concentrate on work. The thought of two whole years without having to think about what to wear and whether this guy or that guy fancies me is sheer heaven."

Laura looked at Chelsea.

Chelsea looked at Jemma.

They shrugged.

"It's your life, I suppose," said Laura doubtfully.

"Are you sure?" asked Chelsea.

"Oh yes," said Sumitha. "I've never been so sure of anything in my life."

"But what about your love life?" persisted Jemma.

"It can wait," said Sumitha. "And, besides, I rather think it may turn up just where I least expected it."

WHERE DO WE GO FROM HERE?

"Sumitha!" probed Laura. "What are you getting at?"

"I'm saying nothing," said Sumitha. "Nothing at all. For now."

Don't Be Naff...

A levels: high school diploma

Agony Aunt/Uncle: advice columnist

BBC: British Broadcasting Corp.

Bin: garbage

Brill: brilliant, wonderful

Bunk off: skip school

Chemist: drug store

Chuffed: psyched, smugly pleased

Comprehensive: public school

Crèche: daycare, nursery

Cred: reputation

Crisps: potato chips

Daft: stupid

Fifth form: eleventh grade

Flat: apartment

GCSEs: senior exams to pass eleventh grade

Get knotted: get lost

Get into a strop: have a fit

Get off: make out, neck

Gobsmacked: shocked

Go spare: freak out

Grotty: gross, dirty

Half-term: school break

Home and dry: in the clear

Kit: gear

Knickers: underwear

Loo: bathroom

Mad: crazy

Made redundant: fired, laid off

Mate: friend

Mizz: miserable

Mocks: mock exams for GSCEs

Muck in: get into the thick of things

Suss Out the Words!

Naff: cheesy

On the dole: unemployed

Panto: pantomime

Playing truant: skipping school

Poxy: disgusting

Prat: fool

Public school: private school

Queue: line

Reading the stars: reading horoscopes

Revision: studying for tests and exams

Row: fight

Rubbish: garbage

Ruck: scuffle, fight

Rucksack: backpack

Scratty: gross, tattered

Semi: semi-detached house

Sixth form: twelfth grade

Snog: make out

Suss: find, figure out

Swot: nerd, brain

Swot up: study

Uni: university

Up sticks: pick up and leave

Wally: dork

Wet: feeble, clueless

Weed: wimp

Yonks: ages

God I have a piece of paper